RICK STEIN

my favourite seafood recipes

This edition created by BBC Worldwide Limited for Marks and Spencer 2002

The recipes contained in this book first appeared in the following titles: *Taste of the Sea*, which was originally published by BBC Worldwide in 1995 (photographs by Graham Kirk), *Fruits of the Sea*, which was originally published by BBC Worldwide in 1997 (photographs by Laurie Evans), *Rick Stein Cooks Fish*, which was originally published by BBC Worldwide in 1997 (photographs by Philip Webb), *Rick Stein Cooks Seafood*, which was originally published in 1998 (photographs by Juliet Piddington), *Seafood Odyssey*, which was originally published by BBC Worldwide in 1999 (photographs by James Murphy) and *Seafood Lovers' Guide*, which was originally published in 2000 (photographs by James Murphy).
The following recipes have previously appeared in BBC *Good Food Magazine* in their feature, *Rick Stein's Guide to British Fish: Grilled Lemon Sole with a Roasted Red Pepper Butter, Chilli-glazed Rainbow Trout with Bok Choy, Grilled Salmon with Curly Kale and a Noilly Prat Sauce, Tiger Prawn and Avocado Salad* (all photographed by David Munns).

ISBN 0 563 48837 9

Commissioning Editor: Vivien Bowler
Project Editor: Rachel Copus
Design Manager: Sarah Ponder
Designer: Kathryn Gammon
Home Economists: Debbie Major, Louise Pickford, Sarah Ramsbottom and Fran Ward
Typographic Styling: Paul Welti
Picture Researcher: Claire Parker
Production Controller: Belinda Rapley

Printed and bound in England by Butler and Tanner Ltd, Frome, Somerset
Jacket and laminated case printed by Lawrence-Allen Ltd, Weston-Super-Mare
Colour origination by Radstock Reproductions Ltd, Midsomer Norton

Cover photograph by James Murphy: *Grlled Dublin Bay Prawns with a Pernod and Olive Oil Dressing* (page 120)

MARKS &
SPENCER

RICK STEIN

my favourite seafood recipes

contents

introduction

When Marks and Spencer first asked me to put together a selection of my favourite fish recipes I was extremely pleased. I leafed through my previous books including *Taste of the Sea*, *Fruits of the Sea* and *Seafood Odyssey*, all books published to accompany my BBC television series, and rediscovered many old favourites. However, my elation was quickly followed by a touch of dismay at having to limit the number of recipes I chose. There are so many wonderful fish out there and so many recipes that it was a difficult choice. Well, I've done my best and I hope you enjoy the dishes that I've included here.

Since I started my own restaurant in Padstow, Cornwall in 1975 I have witnessed, with amazement, how seafood has grown in popularity. At first I sold grilled plaice and lemon sole, sea bass, mackerel, lobster, crabs, crayfish and the occasional scallop – and that was about it. Now there is literally not a fish that swims in our waters that I can't sell. Some time ago I went out in a trawler and found a species of fish called dragonets in the nets. I brought some back, skinned them, filleted them, deep-fried them, put them on the menu with some chilli sauce and we sold them all that night. I put all of this down to the fact that people are at last beginning to appreciate how bountiful our mackerel-crowded seas are.

Of course, we've also come to realize how good for us fish is and what an important part fish and seafood play in our diet. Fish is what you might call protein without tears, it's completely lean and easily digestible with none of the side-effects of fatty meat. Indeed, it seems clear that oily fish like tuna, trout and salmon might reduce high levels of cholesterol caused by eating too much meat and dairy products. Even non-oily fish, such as mullet, sea bass and squid contain the cholesterol-reducing fish oil known as omega 3.

So I'm optimistic about the future of fish cookery, but we still have a long way to go. There are still many people who are indifferent to seafood. I think that one of the reasons that some of us have been unwilling to cook and try fish is that we don't know what to do with it when we get it. One of the local fishermen describes his favourite way of cooking fish as being to fry them with mushrooms and tomatoes, rather as though he were frying bacon and kidneys. I wouldn't be surprised if the majority of the people in this country considered that to be appetizing. But there is so much more he could do to pass on the excitement and quality of a beautiful fish. Think of roasting the whole fish and serving it with some beurre blanc, or grilling it and serving it with some basil, lemon juice and virgin olive oil with maybe a bit of rough sea salt sprinkled over it.

In *My Favourite Seafood Recipes* I hope I have provided you with a selection of recipes that will persuade you to eat and enjoy more seafood. My recipes, I think, reflect my huge enthusiasm for the subject. Some of them are classic dishes that will be familiar to you, but many have been lovingly collected and brought back from my travels. I hope you enjoy cooking and experimenting with them. Most of all, however, I hope that they fill you full of a passion for fish and fish cookery that will last a lifetime.

Rick Stein

preparation techniques

cleaning round fish
(such as cod, haddock, sea trout, salmon and sardines)

1 Trim the fish by snipping off the fins with kitchen scissors. Working over several sheets of newspaper or under cold running water, remove the scales by scraping the fish from tail to head with a blunt, thick-bladed knife or a fish scaler. With some very delicate-skinned fish, such as sardines, pilchards and small herrings, you can simply rub off the scales with your thumb.

2 To remove the guts, slit open the belly from the anal fin (two-thirds of the way down the fish from the head) up towards the head. Pull out most of the guts with your hand, cut away any pieces of the entrails left behind and then wash out the cavity with plenty of cold water.

3 To remove the gills, pull open the gill flaps and cut them away from the two places where they join the fish, at the back of the head and under the mouth.

cleaning flat fish
(such as sole and plaice)

1 To remove the guts, locate the gut cavity by pressing on the white side of the fish just below the head until you find an area that is much softer. Make a small incision across this area (if you wish to remove any roe at this stage, make a slightly longer incision) and pull out the guts (and roe if you wish) with your little finger. Trim the fish by snipping off the fins with kitchen scissors.

filleting large round fish
(such as cod, haddock, salmon, sea trout and sea bass)

1 Lay the fish on a chopping board and cut closely around the head in a V-shape so that you don't lose too much of the fillet.

2 Lay the fish with its back towards you. Cut along the length of the back, keeping the blade of the knife above the horizontal backbones.

3 Starting at the head, cut the fillet away from the bones, keeping the blade as close to them as you can. Once you have released some of the fillet, lift it up with your fingers to make it easier to see where you are cutting. When you near the rib bones which surround the intestines, if they are thick enough, cut as close to them as you can (with hake, for example); if very fine, cut through them and then remove the bones from the fillet with tweezers afterwards. Turn the fish over and repeat on the other side.

filleting small round fish
(such as sardines and trout)

1 Lay the fish on a chopping board with its back towards you. Cut around the back of the head, through the flesh of the fillet down to the backbone.

2 Turn the knife towards the tail and, beginning just behind the head, carefully start to cut the fillet away from the bones, down towards the belly.

preparing prawns

3 Once you have loosened enough flesh to enable you to get the whole blade of the knife underneath the fillet, rest a hand on top of the fish and cut away the fillet in one clean sweep right down to the tail, keeping the blade close to the bones as you do so. Remove any small bones left in the fillet with a pair of tweezers. Turn the fish over and repeat on the other side.

2 Starting where the backbone meets the head, slide the blade of the knife under the corner of one of the fillets. Carefully cut it away from the bones, folding the released fillet back as you do so. Keep the blade of the knife almost flat and as close to the bones as possible. Remove the adjacent fillet in the same way. Turn the fish over and repeat on the other side.

2 Flip the flap of fish over. Firmly take hold of the skin and, working away from you, continue to cut along its length, sawing with the knife from side to side and keeping the blade of the knife close against the skin.

1 Firmly twist the head away from the body and discard, or use for stock. Turn the prawn over and break open the soft shell along the belly, then carefully peel it away from the flesh. For some recipes you may wish to leave the tail section in place.

filleting flat fish

skinning fillets of fish

cleaning mussels

1 You will get 4 fillets from 1 flat fish. Lay the fish on a chopping board and cut around the back of the head and across the tail. Then cut through the skin down the centre of the fish, very slightly to one side of the raised backbone, working from the head down to the tail.

1 Place the fillet, skin-side down, on a chopping board, with the narrowest (tail) end nearest to you. Angling the blade of the knife down towards the skin, start to cut between the flesh and the skin until a little flap is released.

1 Wash the mussels in plenty of cold water and scrub the shells with a stiff brush. Use a knife to scrape off any barnacles that are sticking to them.

2 With some large raw prawns you may need to remove the intestinal tract, which looks like a thin black vein running down the back of the prawn flesh. Run the tip of a small knife down the back of the prawn and then lift up and pull out the vein.

2 Discard any open mussels that do not close when lightly tapped on the work surface. Pull out the tough, fibrous beards protruding from the tightly closed shells.

preparing squid

1 Grasp the head in one hand and the body in the other. Gently pull the head and it should come away easily, taking the milky-white intestines with it. You may like to retain the ink sac which will be in the intestines – it will be pearly-white in colour with a slight blue tinge. You can also save the 2 pieces of muscle running down either side of the intestines. The rest of the intestines can be discarded.

2 Cut off the tentacles from the head, then discard the head. Squeeze out the beak-like mouth from the centre of the tentacles, cut it off and discard. The tentacles can either be separated or left intact if very small.

3 Reach into the body and pull out the plastic-like quill and the soft white roe, if there is any.

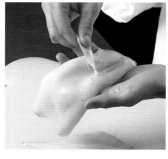

4 Pull off the 2 fins from either side of the body pouch. Then pull away the purple, semi-transparent skin from both the body and the fins. Wash the pouch out with water. If the pouch is too long and narrow for you to reach right down inside when cleaning (and you are not planning to stuff it), a trick for cleaning it out thoroughly is to cut off the very tip and then wash it out with running water, squeezing out any residue as you do so.

preparing scallops

1 Wash the scallops in plenty of cold water. Hold the scallop flat-shell uppermost and slide the blade of a filleting knife between the shells. Keeping the blade flat against the top shell, feel for the ligament that joins the shell to the muscle meat of the scallop and cut through it.

2 Lift off the top shell and pull out the black stomach sac and the frilly 'skirt', which surrounds the white scallop meat and bright orange coral. Cut the scallop meat away from the bottom shell.

3 Pull off and discard the small white ligament that is attached to the side of the scallop meat.

1

cod & haddock dishes

roast cod with aïoli and butterbeans ▪ **fish and chips** with tartare sauce ▪ **grilled cod** with laksa noodles and sambal blachan ▪ **fillet of cod** with saffron mashed potatoes ▪ **deep-fried cod** stuffed with pesto butter ▪ **classic cod** in parsley sauce ▪ **cod with red wine sauce** ▪ **grilled cod** with lettuce hearts and a rich chicken and tarragon dressing ▪ **baked cod portuguese** ▪ **cod niçoise** ▪ **fish pie** ▪ **ravioli of creamed cod** with rocket pesto ▪ **grilled salted cod** with beer, bacon and cabbage ▪ **grilled cod** with green split peas and tartare sauce ▪ **eggs benedict** with smoked haddock ▪ **smoked haddock** with savoy cabbage, lemon and noisette butter ▪ **omelette arnold bennett** ▪ **cullen skink** ▪ **mild potato curry** topped with smoked haddock and a poached egg ▪ **steamed haddock** on buttered leeks with grain mustard sauce ▪ **broiled haddock** fillets with succotash ▪ **poached haddock** with mussels, spinach and chervil ▪ **haddock and cornish yarg pie** with a potato pastry crust ▪ **smoked haddock kedgeree**

roast cod with aïoli and butterbeans

This is a hot version of the classic Provençal dish *aïoli garni*. Here, a fillet of cod is served roasted with sea salt and is accompanied by garlic mayonnaise, butterbeans, fennel and a fish *fumet* flavoured with basil.

SERVES 4

50 G (2 OZ) BUTTERBEANS

2 EGGS

1 BULB OF FENNEL

4 x 175-200 G (6-7 OZ) PIECES OF UNSKINNED THICK COD FILLET

MELTED BUTTER, FOR BRUSHING

1 TEASPOON SEA SALT

FRESHLY GROUND BLACK PEPPER

1 QUANTITY *AÏOLI* (SEE P. 141)

FOR THE SAUCE:

225 G (8 OZ) CHOPPED MIXED CARROT, LEEK, CELERY AND ONION

50 G (2 OZ) UNSALTED BUTTER

1 TABLESPOON COGNAC

10 G (¼ OZ) DRIED MUSHROOMS

1 TABLESPOON BALSAMIC VINEGAR

¼ RED CHILLI, SEEDED AND CHOPPED

2 TABLESPOONS OLIVE OIL

1 TEASPOON THAI FISH SAUCE *(NAM PLA)*

600 ML (1 PINT) *FISH STOCK* (SEE P. 140)

½ TEASPOON SALT

4 BASIL LEAVES, FINELY SLICED

METHOD

For the sauce, sweat the mixture of carrot, leek, celery and onion in a large pan with half the butter, until soft. Add the cognac and let it boil, then add all the rest of the sauce ingredients, except the remaining butter and basil leaves. Simmer for 30 minutes, then pass through a fine sieve. Bring the sauce back to the boil and simmer until it has reduced to about 150 ml (5 fl oz).

Bring the butterbeans to the boil in a large pan of salted water. Simmer gently until very soft. Remove from the heat and keep warm in the cooking liquid. Hard-boil the eggs for 8 minutes. Drain, remove the shells and keep warm.

Remove the outer leaves of the fennel but don't cut off the tops. Slice into thin sections, then cook in salted water until just tender. Drain and keep warm.

Pre-heat the oven to 230°C/450°F/Gas 8. Brush the pieces of cod with melted butter and season with salt and pepper. Roast the cod, skin-side up, in the oven until just cooked through (this will take 10–15 minutes). Place on 4 warmed plates. Drain the butterbeans and divide between the plates. Add the fennel, cut the eggs in half and put one half on each plate, then add a spoonful of aïoli to each serving.

Bring the sauce to the boil and whisk in the last 25 g (1 oz) of butter, then add the basil leaves. Pour the sauce over the butterbeans, egg and fennel and serve.

fish and chips with tartare sauce

The best ever! I used to think that the only decent chips were the thin and crispy French-style *frites* because my experiences of chips in British fish and chip shops have been rather limp and soggy. But one day, while walking down London's King's Road, I nipped into a place called Ed's Easy Diner. I had a burger and a side order of American fries, which were big, thick chips and were 'to die for'. They were crisp and fat but slightly grainy and sandy on the outside, like the best roast potatoes. I hope I've managed to re-create them here.

SERVES 4

900 G (2 LB) MARIS PIPER POTATOES, PEELED AND CUT LENGTHWAYS
    INTO CHIPS 1 CM (½ IN) THICK
SUNFLOWER OIL, FOR DEEP-FRYING
4 X 175 G (6 OZ) PIECES OF THICK COD FILLET, TAKEN FROM THE LOIN END,
    NOT THE TAIL, SKINNED (SEE P. 7)
SALT AND FRESHLY GROUND BLACK PEPPER
1 QUANTITY *TARTARE SAUCE* (SEE P. 141)

FOR THE BATTER:
240 G (8½ OZ) PLAIN FLOUR
1 TEASPOON SALT
3½ TEASPOONS BAKING POWDER
270 ML (9 FL OZ) ICE COLD WATER

METHOD

For the batter, mix the flour, salt and baking powder with the water. Keep cold and use within 20 minutes of making.

Pre-heat the oven to 150°C/300°F/Gas 2. Line a baking tray with plenty of kitchen paper and set aside.

Pour some sunflower oil into a large, deep pan until it is about a third full and heat it to 130°C/260°F. Drop half the chips into a frying basket and cook them for about 5 minutes, until tender when pierced with the tip of a knife but not coloured. Lift them out and drain off excess oil. Repeat with the rest of the chips and set aside.

To fry the fish, heat the oil to 160°C/325°F, season the pieces of fish with salt and pepper and then dip them into the batter. Fry 2 pieces for 7–8 minutes, until crisp and a deep golden brown. Lift out and drain on the paper-lined tray, then keep hot in the oven while you cook the other 2 pieces.

Now raise the temperature of the oil to 190°C/375°F and cook the chips in small batches for about 2 minutes, until they are crisp and golden. Lift them out of the pan and give them a good shake to remove the excess oil, then drain on kitchen paper and keep them hot while you cook the rest. Sprinkle with salt and serve them with the deep-fried cod and tartare sauce.

grilled cod with laksa noodles
and sambal blachan

The idea behind this dish is straightforward. Take a lovely thick fillet of grilled cod and set it on top of a spice and coconut laksa with egg noodles, so the soft delicate cod flakes taste sweet against the fiery fragrance of coconut and chilli.

SERVES 4

120 ML (4 FL OZ) SUNFLOWER OIL, PLUS EXTRA FOR BRUSHING

450 ML (15 FL OZ) *CHICKEN STOCK* (SEE P. 140) OR *FISH STOCK* (SEE P. 140)

4 x 175-225 G (6-8 OZ) PIECES OF UNSKINNED THICK COD FILLET

50 G (2 OZ) DRIED MEDIUM EGG NOODLES

400 ML (14 FL OZ) COCONUT MILK

100 G (4 OZ) FRESH BEANSPROUTS

4 SPRING ONIONS, THINLY SLICED ON THE DIAGONAL

SALT AND FRESHLY GROUND BLACK PEPPER

A HANDFUL OF CHOPPED MIXED MINT, BASIL AND CORIANDER

1 LIME, CUT INTO 4 WEDGES

FOR THE *SAMBAL BLACHAN*:

2 KAFFIR LIME LEAVES (OPTIONAL)

8 RED FINGER CHILLIES, SLICED

1 TEASPOON SALT

1 TEASPOON DRIED SHRIMP PASTE (*BLACHAN*)

ZEST AND JUICE OF 1 LIME

FOR THE LAKSA SPICE PASTE:

25 G (1 OZ) DRIED SHRIMPS

3 RED FINGER CHILLIES, ROUGHLY CHOPPED

2 LEMONGRASS STALKS, OUTER LEAVES REMOVED AND THE CORES
   ROUGHLY CHOPPED

25 G (1 OZ) CANDLENUTS OR UNROASTED CASHEW NUTS

2 GARLIC CLOVES

2.5 CM (1 IN) FRESH ROOT GINGER, ROUGHLY CHOPPED

1 TEASPOON TURMERIC POWDER

1 SMALL ONION, ROUGHLY CHOPPED

1 TEASPOON GROUND CORIANDER

JUICE OF 1 LIME

2 TABLESPOONS COLD WATER (OR ENOUGH TO MAKE A SMOOTH PASTE)

METHOD

For the *sambal blachan*, if using lime leaves, remove the spines and shred the leaves very finely. Put them in a food processor with the chillies, salt, shrimp paste, lime zest and juice and blend to a coarse paste. Spoon into a serving bowl.

For the laksa spice paste, cover the dried shrimps with warm water and leave them to soak for 15 minutes. Drain and put into a food processor with the rest of the ingredients. Blend to a smooth paste.

Heat the oil in a large pan, add the laksa paste and fry for 10 minutes, stirring constantly, until it smells very fragrant. Add the stock and simmer for 10 minutes.

Pre-heat the grill to high. Brush both sides of the cod with a little sunflower oil and season with some salt and pepper. Place on a lightly oiled baking tray, skin-side up, and grill for 8 minutes.

Meanwhile, drop the noodles into a pan of boiling salted water, cover and remove from the heat. Leave to soak for 4 minutes, then drain. Add the coconut milk to the stock mixture and simmer for 3 minutes. Add the noodles, beansprouts, spring onions and 1 teaspoon of salt.

To serve, spoon the laksa into 4 large warmed soup plates and place a piece of cod in the centre of each. Scatter the chopped mint, basil and coriander around the edge and then spoon a little of the *sambal blachan* over the cod. Serve the rest separately, with the lime wedges.

fillet of cod with saffron mashed potatoes

This dish is known in our kitchen as cod and saff mash. I got the idea for the potatoes from Simon Hopkinson, the chef and food writer, whose recipes in the *Independent* are not only a pleasure to read but also usually leave me thinking, blast, I wish I'd come up with that one. Cod with saff mash not only has this delightful purée of potatoes with saffron and olive oil, but also a mayonnaise-based sauce flavoured with tomato, orange and chilli and, on the side, some tapenade, which is a purée of black olives, anchovy and capers. There is a recipe for tapenade on page 142 but you can buy jars of good-quality tapenade in all the major supermarkets these days, so feel free to buy a jar if you don't have time to make your own.

SERVES 4

4 x 175 G (6 OZ) PIECES OF UNSKINNED THICK COD FILLET

OLIVE OIL FOR BRUSHING

COARSE SEA SALT AND FRESHLY GROUND BLACK PEPPER

2 TOMATOES, SKINNED, SEEDED AND DICED

1 TABLESPOON CHOPPED PARSLEY

ABOUT 8 TEASPOONS *TAPENADE* (SEE P. 142)

FOR THE SAUCE:

50 G (2 OZ) CARROT, VERY FINELY CHOPPED

50 G (2 OZ) ONION, VERY FINELY CHOPPED

½ RED CHILLI, SEEDED AND VERY FINELY CHOPPED

5 CM (2 IN) PIECE OF PARED ORANGE ZEST

1 TABLESPOON OLIVE OIL

JUICE OF ½ ORANGE

50 ML (2 FL OZ) WHITE WINE

1 TOMATO, CHOPPED

600 ML (1 PINT) *FISH STOCK* (SEE P. 140)

4 TABLESPOONS *MAYONNAISE* (SEE P. 141) MADE WITH OLIVE OIL

SALT AND WHITE PEPPER

FOR THE POTATOES:

900 G (2 LB) FLOURY POTATOES, PEELED AND CUT INTO CHUNKS

A GOOD PINCH OF SAFFRON

½ GARLIC CLOVE, CRUSHED

50 ML (2 FL OZ) OLIVE OIL

25 ML (1 FL OZ) DOUBLE CREAM

METHOD

For the sauce, fry the carrot, onion and chilli with the orange zest in the olive oil for 5 minutes. Add the orange juice, white wine, tomato and stock and simmer for 20 minutes. Season with salt and white pepper.

Meanwhile, put the potatoes in a pan and barely cover with cold water. Add the saffron and a pinch of salt, then bring to the boil and cook for 20 minutes or until tender. Drain the cooking liquid off the potatoes into a clean pan and boil rapidly until reduced to 4–6 tablespoons. Mash the potatoes until smooth, then beat in the reduced cooking liquid, garlic, olive oil, cream and some salt and pepper to taste. Keep warm.

Strain the sauce into a jug. Put the mayonnaise in a small pan and gradually whisk in the sauce. Cook over a very gentle heat until it thickens and just coats the back of a spoon. Do not let it boil or it will curdle. Keep warm.

Pre-heat the grill to high. Brush both sides of the cod with olive oil and season with coarse sea salt and pepper. Place on the oiled rack of the grill pan, skin-side up, and cook for 8 minutes.

To serve, put the saffron mashed potatoes in the centre of 4 warmed plates and place the cod on top. Pour the sauce around the edge and sprinkle with the diced tomato and chopped parsley. Put 2 small teaspoons of the tapenade on either side of each plate.

deep-fried cod stuffed with pesto butter

The contrast between a crisp, golden breadcrumb coating, delicate flakes of moist white fish and a just-melted centre of fragrant basil, garlic and pine kernel pesto is a delight. It is important to get the right cut of fish for this dish. A good thick fillet of cod cut from just behind the head of a large fish is ideal.

SERVES 4

1 x 1.25 KG (2½ LB) PIECE OF THICK COD FILLET, SKINNED (SEE P. 7)

40 G (1½ OZ) PLAIN FLOUR, SEASONED WITH SALT AND PEPPER

1 LARGE EGG, BEATEN

75 G (3 OZ) FRESH WHITE BREADCRUMBS

SUNFLOWER OIL, FOR DEEP-FRYING

FOR THE PESTO BUTTER:

15 G (½ OZ) BASIL

2 LARGE GARLIC CLOVES, ROUGHLY CHOPPED

15 G (½ OZ) FRESHLY GRATED PARMESAN CHEESE

15 G (½ OZ) PINE KERNELS

3 TABLESPOONS OLIVE OIL

½ TEASPOON SALT

25 G (1 OZ) BUTTER, SOFTENED

METHOD

First make the pesto butter. Put all the ingredients except the butter into a food processor and blend until smooth. Scrape the mixture into a bowl and beat in the softened butter. Spoon the pesto butter on to a sheet of cling film in a line about 10 cm (4 in) long, then roll it up in the cling film into a sausage shape, twisting the ends of the cling film to secure it. Put in the freezer until hard. When the butter is firm, use to stuff the fish (see below).

Pour the oil into a large pan so that it is about one-third full. Heat to 180°C/350°F or until a small piece of white bread dropped into the oil browns and rises to the surface in 1 minute. Dip the pieces of fish in the seasoned flour, making sure that they are all well coated. Then dip them into the beaten egg and lastly the breadcrumbs, pressing them on well to give a thick, even coating. Deep-fry the fish, 2 pieces at a time, for 5 minutes or until crisp and golden. Lift out and drain on kitchen paper, then serve straight away.

Sun-dried tomato, roasted red pepper and chilli butter:

Finely chop half a roasted red pepper, 2 sun-dried tomatoes and half a red finger chilli, then mix together with a little salt. Beat in 25 g (1 oz) of softened butter, then continue as for the main recipe.

stuffing cod with pesto butter

1 Trim away the thinner belly flap from the fillet and cut the rest into four 175 g (6 oz) pieces, each about 12.5 cm (5 in) long.

2 To make a pocket in the pieces of cod, make a deep cut, 7.5 cm (3 in) long, in the side of each piece of fish with a small, sharp knife, taking care not to cut right through to the other side.

3 Remove the butter from the freezer, unwrap and cut into slices 1 cm (½ in) thick. Gently poke 2 pieces of butter into the pocket of each piece of fish and then close up the pocket so that no butter is visible.

classic cod in parsley sauce

If you tried to think of one of the most mundane-sounding English dishes, it would probably be cod in parsley sauce. Most of us have childhood memories of cod with parsley sauce and it was with this in mind that I decided to make it to see if it really is as boring as it is made out to be. I made a good, but simple, parsley sauce to go with a fresh piece of cod. It was like a sunny day proving that with English food, as long as the raw materials are the best, simplicity is everything.

SERVES 4

1 SLICE OF LEMON

1 TABLESPOON SALT

750–900 G (1½–2 LB) PIECE OF UNSKINNED THICK COD FILLET

25 G (1 OZ) UNSALTED BUTTER

15 G (½ OZ) PLAIN FLOUR

300 ML (1 PINT) FULL-CREAM MILK

25 G (1 OZ) PARSLEY, STALKS REMOVED, CHOPPED

METHOD

Put the lemon and salt in a large pan with 2.25 litres (4 pints) of water. Bring to the boil then simmer for 5 minutes. Add the cod and simmer for 2 minutes. Remove the pan from the heat and leave the cod to finish cooking gently in the cooking liquid.

Melt 25 g (1 oz) of the butter in a heavy-based pan and sprinkle over the flour. Stir continuously with a wooden spoon to mix, then cook until the mixture smells nutty. Gradually pour in the milk, stirring all the time, to make a smooth sauce. Add 300 ml (10 fl oz) of the fish-cooking liquid and leave to simmer for at least 20 minutes.

Drain the cod and cut into 4 portions. Place on 4 warmed plates. Stir the parsley and the rest of the butter into the sauce and coat the fish liberally with it. Serve with some potatoes boiled in salted water and a sprig of mint.

cod with red wine sauce

This dish originated from one of the best restaurants in the world, Giradet at Crisser, near Lausanne in Switzerland. I got the recipe from a book that has given me a great deal of pleasure, Egon Ronay's *The Great Dishes In My Life*. Almost better than an autobiography, it's one of those books that everyone who has influenced the way we eat should write. The original recipe calls for a very elaborate fish-scale effect to be made with wafer-thin slices of small potatoes, which are fried and laid on top of the fish. We occasionally do this at the restaurant but it really is three-star cooking and probably, I think, outside the scope of even an advanced cookery book like this!

A good accompaniment to the cod would be some courgettes fried very gently in butter with chopped tarragon and chives.

SERVES 4

75 G (3 OZ) UNSALTED BUTTER

4 x 175 G (6 OZ) PIECES OF UNSKINNED THICK COD FILLET

50 G (2 OZ) CARROT, CHOPPED

50 G (2 OZ) CELERY, CHOPPED

50 G (2 OZ) ONION, CHOPPED

A SMALL PINCH OF GROUND ALLSPICE

A SMALL PINCH OF GROUND CLOVES

A SMALL PINCH OF GRATED NUTMEG

A LARGE PINCH OF CURRY POWDER

600 ML (1 PINT) RED WINE

600 ML (1 PINT) *CHICKEN STOCK* (SEE P. 140)

1 TEASPOON SUGAR

1 TABLESPOON PLAIN FLOUR

COARSE SEA SALT AND FRESHLY GROUND BLACK PEPPER

FOR THE LENTILS:

50 G (2 OZ) DRIED PUY LENTILS

300 ML (10 FL OZ) *FISH STOCK* (SEE P. 140)

1 CLOVE

1 BAY LEAF

2 SLICES OF ONION, PEELED

½ TEASPOON SALT

METHOD

Put all the ingredients for the lentils into a pan and simmer until tender. Drain, remove the clove and bay leaf, then cover and keep warm.

Melt 50 g (2 oz) of the butter in a medium-sized pan and brush a little over the cod. Season the fish on both sides with salt and a little pepper and put, skin-side up, on a greased baking tray.

For the sauce, add the carrot, celery, onion and spices to the melted butter in the pan and fry over a high heat for about 10 minutes, until the vegetables are well browned. Add the red wine, chicken stock, sugar and ¼ teaspoon of salt, bring to the boil and boil until reduced to 175 ml/6 fl oz and well concentrated in flavour. Strain the reduced sauce into a clean pan and keep warm.

Pre-heat the grill to high. Grill the cod for 8 minutes, until the skin is well browned. Meanwhile, mix the remaining 25 g/1 oz of butter with the flour to make a smooth paste. Bring the sauce to the boil and then whisk in the paste, a little at a time. Simmer for 2 minutes until the sauce is smooth and thickened. Adjust the seasoning if necessary.

To serve, put the lentils on 4 warmed plates and place the cod on top. Spoon the sauce around the edge of the plate.

grilled cod with lettuce hearts and a rich chicken and tarragon dressing

I am addicted to warm fish salads and this is essentially that. I love the soft taste of white flakes of cod against crisp lettuce and *al dente* asparagus. The salad is finished with a dressing made with some good chicken stock that has been reduced with tarragon and garlic until it is beautifully concentrated.

SERVES 4

550 G (1¼ LB) PIECE OF THICK COD FILLET, SKINNED (SEE P. 7)

1.2 LITRES (2 PINTS) *CHICKEN STOCK* (SEE P. 140)

A FEW TARRAGON STALKS

2 GARLIC CLOVES

2 TABLESPOONS EXTRA VIRGIN OLIVE OIL

100 G (4 OZ) ASPARAGUS TIPS

4 SOFT ROUND LETTUCES

12 VERY THIN SLICES OF PANCETTA

1 TEASPOON CHOPPED CHIVES

1 TEASPOON CHOPPED TARRAGON

1½ TEASPOONS WHITE WINE VINEGAR

SALT AND FRESHLY GROUND BLACK PEPPER

METHOD

Put the cod into a shallow dish and sprinkle liberally with salt. Set aside for 20 minutes. Meanwhile, put the chicken stock, tarragon stalks and garlic cloves into a large pan and boil until reduced to about 85 ml (3 fl oz) and nicely concentrated in flavour. Strain into a small clean pan and keep warm.

Rinse the salt off the fish and dry well on kitchen paper. Brush with a little of the olive oil, season with some pepper and place on a lightly oiled baking tray.

Cook the asparagus tips in boiling salted water until just tender. Drain, refresh and keep warm. Remove the outside leaves from each lettuce until you get down to the pale green hearts. Cut each one into quarters.

Pre-heat the grill to high, then grill the cod for about 10–12 minutes. Put the slices of pancetta over the fish and grill for 1–2 minutes, until it is crisp and lightly golden.

Put the quartered lettuce hearts in the centre of 4 warmed plates. Break the pancetta into small pieces and the cod into chunky flakes. Arrange the cod around the lettuce with the pancetta and asparagus. Sprinkle over the chopped chives and tarragon. Spoon the warm chicken stock over the lettuce and a little over the rest of the plate. Whisk the remaining olive oil, the vinegar and some salt and pepper together, drizzle over the plate and serve straight away.

baked cod portuguese

I have never eaten a cod Portuguese that was anything other than fish in a watery sauce, so I thought it would be fun to take such a standard dish and try and restore it to something like the original. The problem with cooking many Portuguese or Mediterranean dishes in Britain is that they never taste the same using vegetables, particularly tomatoes, that have been grown in northern Europe. You have to zip up these dishes with something to compensate for the lack of sunshine in the vegetables. I have added sun-dried tomatoes to boost the flavour and used fresh plum tomatoes for authenticity.

SERVES 4

75 G (3 OZ) UNSALTED BUTTER

4 x 175–225 G (6–8 OZ) PIECES OF UNSKINNED THICK COD FILLET

1 LARGE ONION, CUT INTO QUARTERS AND FINELY SLICED

4 PLUM TOMATOES, SKINNED, SEEDED AND CHOPPED

4 SUN-DRIED TOMATOES IN OIL, DRAINED AND FINELY CHOPPED

300 ML (10 FL OZ) *FISH STOCK* (SEE P. 140)

120 ML (4 FL OZ) WHITE WINE

2 TABLESPOONS CHOPPED PARSLEY

SALT AND FRESHLY GROUND BLACK PEPPER

SPRIGS OF PARSLEY, TO GARNISH

METHOD

Melt half the butter in a shallow flameproof casserole dish that is big enough to hold all the pieces of cod in a single layer. Fry the cod, skin-side down, for 1 minute, until crisp and golden. Carefully remove from the casserole and set aside.

Add the onion to the casserole and fry gently for 5 minutes, until softened. Add the plum tomatoes, sun-dried tomatoes, stock and white wine. Bring to the boil and simmer for 10 minutes, until slightly reduced and thickened.

Pre-heat the oven to 200°C/400°F/Gas 6.

Place the cod, skin-side up, on top of the onion and tomato mixture, transfer the casserole to the oven and bake for 5–6 minutes – less if the pieces of cod are thin. Remove from the oven and lift the cod out on to a warm plate. Return the casserole to the stove over a high heat, add the remaining butter and reduce by boiling rapidly for about 4 minutes, stirring now and then, to make a really thick sauce. Stir in the parsley, season with salt and pepper and cook for 30 seconds more. Spoon the sauce on to 4 warmed plates, put the cod on top and garnish with sprigs of parsley. Serve with boiled potatoes and a green salad.

cod niçoise

This recipe is from a rather memorable competition set by the *Radio Times* magazine, where readers were asked to impress me with their fish cookery. The finalists' recipes were indeed extremely impressive and Janine Lishman-Peat's recipe was one I might well have written myself except that she thought of it and I probably never would.

SERVES 4

600 G (1 LB 6 OZ) CHARLOTTE POTATOES OR OTHER LARGE, WAXY NEW
  POTATOES, SCRAPED IF VERY NEW

OLIVE OIL, FOR GRILLING

4 x 175–225 G (6–8OZ) PIECES OF UNSKINNED THICK COD FILLET

4–6 TABLESPOONS *MAYONNAISE* (SEE P. 141) MADE WITH HALF SUNFLOWER,
  HALF OLIVE OIL AND LEMON JUICE INSTEAD OF VINEGAR

50 G (2 OZ) BABY SALAD LEAVES

4 TABLESPOONS *TAPENADE* (SEE P. 142)

SALT

SPRIGS OF PARSLEY OR BASIL, TO GARNISH

FOR THE TOMATO SAUCE:

150 G (5 OZ) CHERRY TOMATOES

1 TABLESPOON SUN-DRIED TOMATO PASTE

1 TABLESPOON TOMATO PURÉE

2 TEASPOONS CASTER SUGAR

METHOD

To make the tomato sauce, purée the tomatoes in a food processor until smooth, press through a sieve to remove the skin and seeds and then return to the cleaned food processor bowl with the sun-dried tomato paste, tomato purée, half the sugar and a pinch of salt. Blend once more and then taste. Add the remaining sugar if you need to, but this will depend on the sweetness and ripeness of the tomatoes. What you should aim for is a sweet and sour taste without any bitterness. Pour the sauce into a bowl.

Cook the potatoes in boiling salted water until tender, then drain and leave until just cool enough to handle.

Meanwhile, heat a ridged cast-iron griddle or frying pan until it is very hot, then brush with a little oil. Rub a little salt into the skin of the cod and place it on the griddle or frying pan, skin-side down. Cook for about 5 minutes until the skin is crisp. Turn over and cook for another 3–4 minutes or until just cooked through.

While the cod is cooking, peel the skins off the warm potatoes (if you haven't already scraped them) and slice them fairly thickly. Spread both sides of each slice with mayonnaise. Arrange in the centre of 4 warmed plates and top with the salad leaves. Rest the cod on top of the leaves. Drizzle a little of the tomato sauce around the edge and then spoon around a little of the tapenade. Garnish with a sprig of parsley or basil.

fish pie

The older I get the keener I am to keep ingredients out of recipes instead of adding them. This is as simple a recipe for fish pie as you can imagine but if the fish is good (and that includes the smoked fish, which must be of the best quality), there is no better fish dish in the world than a British fish pie.

SERVES 4

1 SMALL ONION, THICKLY SLICED

2 CLOVES

1 BAY LEAF

600 ML (1 PINT) MILK

300 ML (10 FL OZ) DOUBLE CREAM

450 G (1 LB) UNSKINNED COD FILLET

225 G (8 OZ) UNDYED SMOKED COD OR HADDOCK FILLET

4 EGGS, PLUS 1 EXTRA YOLK

100 G (4 OZ) BUTTER

45 G (1¾ OZ) PLAIN FLOUR

5 TABLESPOONS CHOPPED FLAT-LEAF PARSLEY

FRESHLY GRATED NUTMEG

1.25 KG (2½ LB) FLOURY POTATOES SUCH AS MARIS PIPER OR
  KING EDWARD, PEELED AND CUT INTO CHUNKS

SALT AND FRESHLY GROUND WHITE PEPPER

METHOD

Stud a couple of the onion slices with the cloves. Put the onion slices in a large pan with the bay leaf, 450 ml (15 fl oz) of the milk, the cream, cod and smoked fish. Bring just to the boil and simmer for 8 minutes. Lift the fish out on to a plate and strain the cooking liquid into a jug. When the fish is cool enough to handle, break it into large flakes, discarding the skin and any bones. Sprinkle it over the base of a shallow 1.75 litre (3 pint) ovenproof dish.

Hard-boil the whole eggs for 8 minutes, then drain and leave to cool. Peel them, cut into chunky slices and arrange on top of the fish.

Melt 50 g (2 oz) of the butter in a pan, add the flour and cook for 1 minute. Take the pan off the heat and gradually stir in the reserved cooking liquid. Return it to the heat and bring slowly to the boil, stirring all the time. Leave it to simmer gently for 10 minutes to cook out the flour. Remove from the heat once more, stir in the parsley and season with nutmeg, salt and pepper. Pour the sauce over the fish and leave to cool. Chill in the fridge for 1 hour.

Boil the potatoes for 15–20 minutes. Drain, mash and add the rest of the butter and the egg yolk. Season with salt and pepper. Beat in enough of the remaining milk to form a soft spreadable mash.

Pre-heat the oven to 200°C/400°F/Gas 6. Spoon the potato over the filling and mark the surface with a fork. Bake for 35–40 minutes, until piping hot and golden brown.

ravioli of creamed cod
with rocket pesto

Commercial salted and dried cod needs long soaking and has a distinctive flavour which is addictive once you are used to it. You can make your own salt cod for this which is easy to make and less assertively flavoured.

SERVES 4 AS A FIRST COURSE

FOR THE EGG PASTA DOUGH:
100 G (4 OZ) PLAIN FLOUR
A LARGE PINCH OF SALT
¼ TEASPOON OLIVE OIL
1 EGG, PLUS 2 EXTRA YOLKS

FOR THE CREAMED COD FILLING:
75 G (3 OZ) PIECE OF UNSKINNED THICK COD FILLET
SALT
25 ML (1 FL OZ) EXTRA VIRGIN OLIVE OIL, PREFERABLY LEMON-FLAVOURED
50 ML (2 FL OZ) DOUBLE CREAM
4 GARLIC CLOVES, SLICED

FOR THE ROCKET PESTO:
85 ML (3 FL OZ) OLIVE OIL
25 G (1 OZ) ROCKET LEAVES, TOUGH STALKS REMOVED
1 GARLIC CLOVE, ROUGHLY CHOPPED
25 G (1 OZ) FINELY GRATED PARMESAN CHEESE
15 G (½ OZ) PINE KERNELS
SALT AND FRESHLY GROUND BLACK PEPPER

FRESHLY SHAVED PARMESAN CHEESE

making ravioli

1 Roll out the pasta dough on a lightly floured work surface into a 38 cm (15 in) square. Then, with your fingertip, make small marks at 3 cm (1½ in) intervals in even rows over one half of the square.

2 Place a teaspoon of the creamed cod filling on each mark.

METHOD

To make your own salt cod, put the cod in a plastic container and completely cover with a thick layer of salt. Refrigerate for 24 hours – the salt will turn to brine overnight.

The next day, remove the cod from the brine and soak it in cold water for 2 hours. If using commercial salt cod, soak in plenty of cold water for 12 hours.

For the pasta dough, put all the ingredients into a bowl and mix together into a ball. Turn out on to a lightly floured surface and knead for about 10 minutes, until smooth and elastic. Wrap in cling film and leave to rest for 10–15 minutes while you make the creamed cod filling. (You can make the pasta up to 2 days in advance: simply wrap it in cling film and place in the fridge.)

Drain the salt cod, put it in a pan and cover with fresh water. Bring to the boil and simmer for 5 minutes. Lift out and, when cool enough to handle, flake the flesh, discarding the skin and any bones.

Put the oil and cream into a small pan and bring to the boil. Put the flaked cod into a food processor with the garlic and the hot cream mixture and blend until smooth. Leave to cool.

For the rocket pesto, put all the ingredients into a food processor and blend until smooth. Scrape into a bowl and set aside.

Make the ravioli (see below). If you are not going to eat them immediately, drop them into a pan of boiling water and cook for just 1 minute. Drop into a bowl of cold water, then lift out and drain. Store in the fridge on oiled trays covered with cling film.

Otherwise, bring 1.75 litres (3 pints) of water to the boil with 1 tablespoon of salt. Add the ravioli and cook for 4 minutes (3 minutes if they have already been blanched). Drain well, then return the ravioli to the pan with the rocket pesto and toss together well. Spoon the ravioli into 4 large warmed pasta plates and serve sprinkled with a few shavings of Parmesan.

3 Brush lines of water between the piles of mixture and then fold over the other half of the square so that the edges meet.

4 Working from the centre of the folded side, outwards and downwards, press firmly around each pile of mixture with your fingers to push out any trapped air and seal in the filling.

5 Trim off the edges of the dough and cut between the rows with a sharp knife or a fluted pasta wheel.

grilled salted cod with beer, bacon and cabbage

This recipe comes from a chef who has sadly left us to run a pub and restaurant in the Home Counties. His name is Jason Fretwell and he was a very inventive chef who was keen on British food. This was one of his best dishes. He also had a great recipe for a steamed fish pudding, which I must get from him some time.

SERVES 4

4 x 175 G (6 OZ) PIECES OF UNSKINNED THICK COD FILLET

50 G (2 OZ) BUTTER

1 SMALL SAVOY CABBAGE, WEIGHING ABOUT 750 G (1½ LB), CORED AND THINLY SLICED

2 TABLESPOONS SUNFLOWER OIL

75 G (3 OZ) RINDLESS SMOKED STREAKY BACON, CUT INTO THIN STRIPS

1 ONION, FINELY CHOPPED

1 GARLIC CLOVE, VERY FINELY CHOPPED

300 ML (10 FL OZ) *CHICKEN STOCK* (SEE P. 140)

300 ML (10 FL OZ) PALE ALE

2 TABLESPOONS CHOPPED PARSLEY, PLUS EXTRA TO GARNISH

SALT AND FRESHLY GROUND BLACK PEPPER

SEA SALT FLAKES

METHOD

Place the cod, skin-side down, on a plate and sprinkle heavily with some salt. Leave for 20 minutes, then rinse the salt off and dry on kitchen paper. Melt 25 g (1 oz) of the butter. Brush the cod with a little of the butter and sprinkle the skin with salt and pepper.

Put the cabbage into a large pan of boiling salted water and bring back to the boil. Drain and refresh under cold running water.

Heat the oil in a large, heavy-based pan, add the bacon and fry over a high heat until crisp and lightly golden. Add the remaining melted butter, onion and garlic and fry for 5 minutes, until the onion is soft and lightly browned. Add the chicken stock and beer to the pan and reduce the volume of liquid by three-quarters over a high heat. Add the cabbage and the rest of the butter and cook gently for a further 5 minutes till the cabbage is tender. Season to taste with salt and pepper, add the parsley and keep warm.

Pre-heat the grill to high. Grill the cod for 8 minutes on one side only, until the skin is crisp and the fish is cooked through. Put the cabbage in 4 large, warmed soup plates. Sprinkle the skin of the cod with some sea salt flakes, pepper and chopped parsley, place on top of the cabbage and serve.

grilled cod with green split peas and tartare sauce

I hope you'll enjoy the way the flakes of cod, the peas and the tartare sauce complement each other. I tested this at our seafood cookery school where I've built a recipe-testing kitchen with a view over the Camel Estuary to Rock. I invited Paul Sellars, the teacher at the school, to come and try it and he said, 'This is what British cooking is all about.' I was delighted with that.

SERVES 4

4 x 225 G (8 OZ) PIECES OF UNSKINNED THICK COD FILLET

50 G (2 OZ) BUTTER, MELTED

1 QUANTITY *TARTARE SAUCE* (SEE P. 141)

SALT AND FRESHLY GROUND BLACK PEPPER

FOR THE GREEN SPLIT PEAS:

450 G (1 LB) GREEN SPLIT PEAS, SOAKED OVERNIGHT

1 ONION, QUARTERED

2 GARLIC CLOVES, PEELED BUT LEFT WHOLE

1 CELERY STICK, HALVED

2 BAY LEAVES

1 SPRIG OF THYME

25 G (1 OZ) BUTTER

METHOD

Drain the split peas and put them into a pan with the onion, garlic, celery, bay leaves and thyme. Cover with 1.2 litres (2 pints) of water, bring to the boil and simmer gently for 1 hour, until the split peas are really tender and most of the liquid has evaporated but the mixture is still quite wet (the peas will continue to absorb the liquid after the cooking time is up).

Lift out and discard the onion, garlic, celery, bay leaves and thyme from the peas and mash the peas briefly with a potato masher to make a coarse paste. Stir in the butter and some seasoning to taste and keep warm.

Pre-heat the grill to high. Brush the pieces of cod with the melted butter and season on both sides with salt and pepper. Place skin-side up on a greased baking tray or the rack of the grill pan and grill for 8–10 minutes, until the skin is crisp and the cod is cooked through. Meanwhile, make sure the split peas are hot and add a little water if necessary to give them a creamy texture.

Serve the cod on top of the peas with the tartare sauce.

eggs benedict with smoked haddock

I'm not usually very keen on taking a well-established dish, replacing some of the ingredients with fish and then calling it something new. But I make the exception for my eggs Benedict because poached eggs and smoked haddock go so well together.

SERVES 4

½ QUANTITY *HOLLANDAISE SAUCE* (SEE P. 140–41)

300 ML (10 FL OZ) MILK

3 BAY LEAVES

2 SLICES OF ONION

6 BLACK PEPPERCORNS

4 x 100 G (4 OZ) PIECES OF UNDYED THICK SMOKED HADDOCK FILLET

1 TABLESPOON WHITE WINE VINEGAR

4 EGGS

2 ENGLISH MUFFINS

COARSELY CRUSHED BLACK PEPPERCORNS AND A FEW CHOPPED CHIVES, TO GARNISH

METHOD

Make the hollandaise sauce and keep it warm, off the heat, over a pan of warm water. Bring the milk and 300 ml (10 fl oz) of water to the boil in a shallow pan. Add the bay leaves, onion, peppercorns and smoked haddock pieces, bring back to a simmer and poach for 4 minutes. Lift the haddock out on to a plate, discard the skin and any bones and keep warm.

Bring about 5 cm (2 in) of water to the boil in a medium-sized pan, add the vinegar and reduce to a gentle simmer. Break the eggs into the pan one at a time and poach for 3 minutes. Meanwhile, slice the muffins in half and toast them until lightly browned. Lift the poached eggs out with a slotted spoon and drain briefly on kitchen paper.

To serve, place the muffin halves on 4 warmed plates and top with the haddock and poached eggs. Spoon over the hollandaise sauce and garnish with a sprinkling of crushed peppercorns and chopped chives.

smoked haddock with savoy
cabbage, lemon and noisette butter

This recipe comes from one of my favourite cookery books, *Bistro Cookery* by Patricia Wells. It is full of the sort of French cooking that we all really love to eat as opposed to the three-star cuisine which is more a matter of impressing us than filling us with love and affection; I love this dish.

SERVES 4

1 SAVOY CABBAGE

750 G (1½ LB) UNDYED SMOKED HADDOCK FILLETS

1 QUANTITY *COURT BOUILLON FOR POACHING SMOKED FISH* (SEE P. 140)

175 G (6 OZ) UNSALTED BUTTER

JUICE OF 1 LEMON

2 TABLESPOONS CHOPPED PARSLEY

SALT AND FRESHLY GROUND BLACK PEPPER

METHOD

Trim the outer leaves of the cabbage then quarter it and remove the thick central core. Thinly slice each quarter and cook in a large pan of boiling, salted water for 10 minutes. Drain and refresh in cold water. Drain again.

Heat the court bouillon to simmering point in a large pan. Add the haddock and cook for 8–12 minutes, according to the thickness of the fillets. Remove from the heat and set aside without draining to keep the fish warm.

Melt half the butter in a large shallow pan over a medium heat. Add the cabbage and cook gently for about 2 minutes to drive off the excess water and concentrate the flavour. Season with salt and pepper. Transfer to a shallow serving dish.

Carefully drain the haddock and discard the skin and any bones. Place the fish on top of the cabbage and keep warm.

In a small pan melt the remaining butter over a medium heat until it turns a pale brown. Remove from the heat, stir in the lemon juice and season with salt and pepper. Spoon the sauce over the haddock, sprinkle on the parsley and serve immediately.

omelette arnold bennett

This is the sort of dish, like eggs Benedict, that I would like to see reappearing on hotel breakfast menus. It's thoroughly agreeable when made using lightly poached smoked haddock, good eggs, cream and Parmesan cheese. There are many versions of this dish, named after the novelist who made the pottery towns of Staffordshire come alive. I must confess I had only read *Anna of the Five Towns* when I filmed the cooking of omelette Arnold Bennett. Now I've read *Clayhanger* and *The Card*, and rediscovered an author who writes so understandingly about the human condition – who writes, as he says, about 'the interestingness of existence'. All that pleasure from one simple omelette from the Savoy.

SERVES 2

300 ML (10 FL OZ) MILK

3 BAY LEAVES

2 SLICES OF ONION

6 BLACK PEPPERCORNS

275 G (10 OZ) UNDYED SMOKED HADDOCK FILLET

6 EGGS

20 G (¾ OZ) UNSALTED BUTTER

2-3 TABLESPOONS DOUBLE CREAM

2 TABLESPOONS FRESHLY GRATED PARMESAN CHEESE

SALT AND FRESHLY GROUND BLACK PEPPER

METHOD

Mix the milk with 300 ml (10 fl oz) of water, pour it into a large shallow pan and bring to the boil. Add the bay leaves, onion slices and peppercorns and bring to the boil. Add the smoked haddock, bring back to a gentle simmer and poach for about 3–4 minutes, until the fish is just cooked. Lift the fish out on to a plate and leave until cool enough to handle, then break it into flakes, discarding the skin and any bones.

Pre-heat the grill to high. Whisk the eggs together with some salt and pepper. Heat a 23–25 cm (9–10 inch) non-stick frying pan over a medium heat, then add the butter and swirl it around to coat the base and sides of the pan. Pour in the eggs and, as they start to set, drag the back of a fork over the base of the pan, lifting up little folds of egg to allow the uncooked egg to run underneath.

When the omelette is set underneath but still very moist on top, sprinkle over the flaked smoked haddock. Pour the cream on top, sprinkle with the Parmesan and put the omelette under the hot grill until lightly golden brown. Slide it on to a warmed plate and serve with a crisp green salad.

cullen skink

When I was writing the recipe for this traditional Scottish smoked haddock soup I was tempted to rename it Smoked Finnan Haddock Soup with Potato, Onions and Parsley, on the grounds that Cullen Skink sounds like something you wouldn't want to give to your pet Jack Russell. But it's a fine Scottish soup of great taste and simplicity. We're all a bit wet in Britain when it comes to naming dishes: if it sounds a bit offputting we call it something else. On the restaurant menu we can never use words such as 'boiled', as in boiled leg of lamb with caper sauce or boiled fish heads, but why not? If that's how you cook the thing, that's how it should be named.

This soup is very easy to prepare. Do make sure that you get the best undyed haddock possible, preferably Finnan haddock, and don't overcook it; the soup really is so much nicer if the flakes of haddock are moist and fresh. Overcooked smoked fish always has a slightly harsh aftertaste. Serve with a chilled Alsace or Gewürztraminer wine.

SERVES 4

2 MEDIUM ONIONS

2 CLOVES

1.2 LITRES (2 PINTS) FULL-CREAM MILK

1 BAY LEAF

225 G (8 OZ) FINNAN SMOKED HADDOCK FILLET OR
    OTHER GOOD-QUALITY UNDYED SMOKED HADDOCK

50 G (2 OZ) BUTTER

350 G (12 OZ) POTATOES, PEELED AND CUT INTO 1 CM (½ IN) DICE

85 ML (3 FL OZ) DOUBLE CREAM

SALT AND FRESHLY GROUND BLACK PEPPER

2 TABLESPOONS ROUGHLY CHOPPED PARSLEY

METHOD

Cut 1 onion in half and stud each half with one of the cloves. Put into a pan with the milk and bay leaf, bring just to the boil and simmer for 5 minutes. Add the fish and simmer for 4–5 minutes or until just firm and opaque – a good guide is to allow 10 minutes per 2.5 cm (1 in) thickness of the fillet. Lift the fish out on to a plate and strain the liquid through a fine sieve into a jug. When the fish is cool enough to handle, discard the skin and any bones. Flake the fish into large pieces and set aside.

Finely chop the remaining onion. Melt the butter in a large pan, add the onion and cook over a gentle heat for 5 minutes, until softened but not browned. Add the reserved milk and the diced potatoes. Bring to the boil, then simmer gently for 10 minutes, until the potatoes are cooked but still just firm.

Blend half the soup in a liquidizer until smooth. Return to the pan with the double cream and flaked haddock, season with a little salt and pepper and warm through for 1–2 minutes. Serve in a warmed soup tureen, scattered with the chopped parsley.

mild potato curry topped with smoked haddock and a poached egg

This dish must be made! The idea of putting spiced potatoes underneath smoked haddock with a poached egg turns a homely English dish into something much more elevated.

Poaching eggs carries the same sort of fear of failure as making omelettes. To avoid any possibility of failure in this recipe I have suggested using a shallow pan and a small amount of water, which should be heated to the merest tremble of a boil. I will always add vinegar to the poaching water, not because it helps the eggs to set but because I like the faint flavour which lingers in the eggs.

SERVES 4

4 x 100 G (4 OZ) PIECES OF UNDYED SMOKED HADDOCK FILLET
2 TEASPOONS WHITE WINE VINEGAR
4 EGGS
SPRIGS OF CORIANDER, TO GARNISH

FOR THE POTATO CURRY:
350 G (12 OZ) WAXY MAIN-CROP POTATOES SUCH AS WILJA,
    PEELED AND CUT INTO 1 CM (½ IN) DICE
2 TABLESPOONS SUNFLOWER OIL
½ TEASPOON YELLOW MUSTARD SEEDS
¼ TEASPOON TURMERIC POWDER
100 G (4 OZ) ONIONS, FINELY CHOPPED
2 TOMATOES, SKINNED AND CHOPPED
1 TEASPOON ROUGHLY CHOPPED CORIANDER
SALT AND FRESHLY GROUND BLACK PEPPER

METHOD

For the potato curry, cook the potatoes in boiling salted water for 6–7 minutes until tender, then drain. Meanwhile, heat the oil in a pan, add the mustard seeds and, when they begin to pop, add the turmeric and onions. Fry for 5 minutes or until the onions are soft and lightly browned. Add the potatoes and some salt and pepper and fry for 1–2 minutes. Add the tomatoes and cook for 1 minute. Stir in the chopped coriander, set aside and keep warm.

Bring about 5 cm (2 in) of water to the boil in a shallow pan. Add the pieces of smoked haddock, bring back to a simmer and poach for 4 minutes. Lift out with a slotted spoon, cover and keep warm.

Discard the fish poaching liquid, pour another 5 cm (2 in) of water into the pan and bring to a very gentle simmer; the water should be just trembling and there should be a few bubbles rising up from the bottom of the pan. Add the vinegar, break in the eggs and poach for 3 minutes. Lift out with a slotted spoon and drain briefly on kitchen paper.

To serve, spoon the potato curry into the centre of 4 warmed plates. Remove the skin from each piece of haddock and put the fish on top of the potatoes. Put a poached egg on top of the fish and garnish with coriander sprigs.

steamed haddock on buttered leeks
with grain mustard sauce

Recently I discovered that my book *Taste of the Sea* had been given a *Health Which?* magazine consumer test. They were quite complimentary about the taste and appearance of most of the dishes, and indeed said that some of them were healthy, but they had a right old go at me about my use of butter and cream in others. I must confess to a shred, just a shred of irritation with this point of view. The food police are on to me again. I mean, you're not going to cook this sort of dish every day – it's not exactly staple food – but when you do indulge once in a while, isn't it wonderful? Now in this dish you take three pounds of butter … only joking.

SERVES 4

900 G (2 LB) LARGE LEEKS, TRIMMED AND WASHED
175 G (6 OZ) UNSALTED BUTTER
50 ML (2 FL OZ) DRY WHITE WINE
4 x 175–225 G (6–8 OZ) PIECES OF UNSKINNED HADDOCK FILLET
2 TABLESPOONS WHITE WINE VINEGAR
2 SHALLOTS, ROUGHLY CHOPPED
1 TABLESPOON DOUBLE CREAM
1 TEASPOON WHOLEGRAIN MUSTARD
2 TABLESPOONS CHOPPED PARSLEY
SALT AND FRESHLY GROUND BLACK PEPPER

METHOD

Cut the leeks in half lengthways, then across into pieces 5 cm (2 in) long. Melt 50 g (2 oz) of the butter in a heavy-based pan, add the leeks and cook gently for 3 minutes. Add the wine, 1 teaspoon of salt and some pepper, then cover and cook for 10 minutes, until the leeks are really soft. Keep warm.

Place a trivet or an upturned plate in a large pan. Add about 2.5 cm (1 in) of water and bring to the boil. Place the haddock on a heatproof plate, rest it on the trivet, cover and steam for 8 minutes.

Meanwhile, for the sauce, put the vinegar and shallots into a small pan. Cover and simmer gently for 5 minutes, then take off the lid and boil until almost all the liquid has evaporated. Add the cream, turn the heat down to low and whisk in the remaining butter, a few pieces at a time, until amalgamated into a sauce. Strain through a sieve into a clean pan, stir in the mustard and season to taste with a little salt.

Uncover the leeks and cook over a high heat for a minute or two to drive off all the remaining liquid. Stir in the parsley and then spoon on to 4 warmed plates. Lift the haddock out of the steamer and remove the skin. Put the haddock on top of the leeks, spoon the sauce around and serve.

broiled haddock fillets with succotash

The American word broiled simply means grilled. I've kept it in to add the right atmosphere to the dish. These things matter to me.

Until I went to the Southern states of America I had always thought that succotash was some kind of squash-type vegetable, but it's actually a down-home mix of beans, sweetcorn, bacon and cream, finished with chives. Once I'd made it I knew it was a dead certainty to go with a nice thick fillet of white fish such as haddock. American recipes for succotash normally call for lima beans. These are the same as butterbeans, one name referring to the capital of Peru, where they were first grown, and the other to their buttery, creamy texture.

SERVES 4

175 G (6 OZ) DRIED BUTTERBEANS

100 G (4 OZ) RINDLESS SMOKED STREAKY BACON, IN 1 PIECE

1 SMALL ONION, CHOPPED

1 TABLESPOON SUNFLOWER OIL, IF NEEDED

300 ML (10 FL OZ) *CHICKEN STOCK* (SEE P. 140)

3 EARS OF SWEETCORN

50 ML (2 FL OZ) DOUBLE CREAM

4 x 175-225 G (6-8 OZ) PIECES OF UNSKINNED THICK HADDOCK FILLET

15 G (½ OZ) BUTTER, MELTED

2 TABLESPOONS CHOPPED CHIVES, PLUS A FEW EXTRA FOR GARNISHING

SALT AND FRESHLY GROUND BLACK PEPPER

METHOD

Put the dried butterbeans into a pan and cover with plenty of water. Bring to the boil, then cover, remove from the heat and leave to soak for 2 hours.

Cut the bacon into 5 mm (¼ in) dice, put it into a pan and cook over a low heat until the fat begins to melt. Increase the heat a little and allow it to fry in its own fat until crisp and golden. Add the onion (and the sunflower oil, if it looks a little dry) and cook for about 5 minutes, until soft.

Drain the beans and add them to the pan with the stock. Simmer gently until they are just tender and the stock is well reduced.

Stand the sweetcorn on a chopping board and slice away all the kernels. Add the sweetcorn to the beans with the cream and simmer for 5 minutes.

Meanwhile, pre-heat the grill to high. Brush the pieces of haddock on both sides with the melted butter and season with salt and pepper. Place, skin-side up, on a lightly oiled baking sheet or the rack of the grill pan and grill for 7–8 minutes.

Stir the chives into the beans and season with salt and pepper. Spoon the mixture into 4 warmed soup plates and place the haddock on top. Scatter over a few more chives and serve.

poached haddock with mussels, spinach and chervil

This recipe was a bit of fun for me, summing up my memories and enthusiasm for the east coast of Scotland, where we went out at 3 o'clock one cold morning, long-lining for haddock using mussels as bait. It was a pretty uncomfortable experience, on a rough day in a small open boat on the cold North Sea, talking to two fishermen from Gourdon, Peter and Steven Morrison, who had accents so broad that I could only understand one word in every five. We came back with no haddock, just codling and dabs, and retired to a small bar in Inverbervie to drink Macallan and thaw out from our icy encounter in increasing warmth and good humour. In this dish, you've got the hoped-for haddock, the mussels and the whisky.

SERVES 4

150 G (5 OZ) BUTTER
1 SHALLOT, FINELY CHOPPED
450 G (1 LB) MUSSELS, CLEANED (SEE P. 7)
4 x 175 G (6 OZ) PIECES OF UNSKINNED HADDOCK FILLET
900 G (2 LB) FRESH SPINACH, WASHED, LARGE STALKS REMOVED
1 TABLESPOON MALT WHISKY
1 TEASPOON LEMON JUICE
1 TEASPOON CHOPPED CHERVIL
SALT AND FRESHLY GROUND BLACK PEPPER

METHOD

Heat 25 g (1 oz) of the butter in a 30 cm (12 in) sauté pan, add the shallot and cook gently for 3 minutes, until soft. Meanwhile, put the mussels and 150 ml (5 fl oz) of water into a large pan, cover and cook over a high heat for 3–4 minutes, until the mussels have opened. Tip them into a colander set over a bowl to collect the cooking liquid. When they are cool enough to handle, remove the mussels from all but 8 of the nicest shells. Cover and set aside.

Pour all the mussel liquid except the last tablespoon or two (which will be gritty) into the sauté pan, bring to a simmer and then add the haddock, skin-side up. Cover and simmer gently for 3 minutes. Remove from the heat (leaving the lid in place) and set aside for about 4 minutes to continue cooking.

Meanwhile, melt another 25 g (1 oz) of the butter in a large pan. Add the spinach and stir over a high heat until it has wilted. Cook, stirring briskly, until all the excess liquid has evaporated, then season to taste with some salt and pepper.

Divide the spinach between 4 warmed plates and put the haddock on top. Keep warm. Return the sauté pan to the heat, add the remaining butter and boil rapidly for 3–4 minutes, until the liquid has reduced and emulsified into a sauce. Stir in the whisky and lemon juice and boil for 30 seconds. Add the chervil and mussels and stir for a few seconds, until they have heated through.

Spoon the mussels around the spinach and haddock, dividing the unshelled mussels equally between the plates, then pour over the sauce and serve.

haddock and cornish yarg pie
with a potato pastry crust

Fish pies are always popular. This one is a result of my continuing attempts to try and produce some genuinely local dishes. Here I've used local fish and vegetables and that excellent cheese, Cornish Yarg, which is mild, firm and particularly suited to a pie like this. If you can't get Cornish Yarg, use a mild Cheddar.

SERVES 6

600 ML (1 PINT) MILK

300 ML (10 FL OZ) *FISH STOCK* (SEE P. 140)

750 G (1½ LB) UNSKINNED HADDOCK FILLET

275 G (10 OZ) LEEKS

65 G (2½ OZ) BUTTER

50 G (2 OZ) CARROT, FINELY DICED

50 G (2 OZ) CELERY, FINELY DICED

50 G (2 OZ) ONION, FINELY CHOPPED

40 G (1½ OZ) RINDLESS SMOKED STREAKY BACON, THINLY SLICED

50 G (2 OZ) PLAIN FLOUR

FRESHLY GRATED NUTMEG

100 G (4 OZ) COOKED PEELED PRAWNS

100 G (4 OZ) GRATED CORNISH YARG CHEESE

SALT AND FRESHLY GROUND BLACK PEPPER

FOR THE POTATO PASTRY CRUST:

350 G (12 OZ) POTATOES, PEELED AND CUT INTO CHUNKS

225 G (8 OZ) SELF-RAISING FLOUR

1 TEASPOON SALT

15 TURNS OF THE BLACK PEPPER MILL

175 G (6 OZ) BUTTER, CUT INTO SMALL PIECES

1 EGG, BEATEN

FOR THE BOUQUET GARNI:

1 BAY LEAF

A SMALL BUNCH OF PARSLEY WITH STALKS

LEAVES FROM THE CENTRE OF A HEAD OF CELERY

A SMALL SPRIG OF THYME

METHOD

For the potato pastry, cook the potatoes in boiling salted water until tender. Drain well and either mash or pass through a potato ricer. Leave to cool.

Meanwhile, put the milk and fish stock into a large pan and bring to the boil. Add the haddock and simmer for 5–7 minutes, until firm and opaque. Lift the fish out on to a plate and, when cool enough to handle, break the flesh into large flakes, discarding the skin and any bones.

Clean the leeks, finely dice 50 g (2 oz) of them and set aside. Thinly slice the remainder. Melt 25 g (1 oz) of the butter in a clean pan, add the sliced leeks and fry gently for 2–3 minutes, until just cooked. Lift out with a slotted spoon and set aside.

Add the diced leeks, carrot, celery, onion and bacon to the pan with a little more of the butter if necessary. Fry over a gentle heat for 10 minutes without letting them brown. Add the remaining butter to the vegetables, stir in the flour and cook for 1 minute. Remove the pan from the heat and gradually add the cooking liquid from the haddock, stirring all the time to make a smooth sauce. Bring to the boil, stirring. Tie together all the ingredients for the bouquet garni and add to the pan. Simmer gently for 30 minutes, then remove the bouquet garni from the pan and season the sauce with nutmeg, salt and pepper.

Stir the flaked fish, reserved leeks, prawns and Cornish Yarg into the sauce, spoon into a deep 1.75 litre (3 pint) pie dish and push a pie funnel into the centre of the mixture. Set aside to cool.

Meanwhile, for the pastry, sift the flour, salt and pepper into a bowl. Add the butter and rub it in with your fingertips until the mixture looks like fine breadcrumbs. Add the cold potato and lightly mix into the flour, then add 2 tablespoons of cold water and stir with a round-bladed knife until everything starts to stick together. Form it into a ball, turn out on to a lightly floured work surface and knead briefly until smooth. Chill for 20–30 minutes.

Pre-heat the oven to 200°C/400°F/Gas 6. Roll out the pastry on a floured surface until it is slightly larger than the top of the pie dish. Cut a strip off the edge of the pastry, brush with a little water and press it on to the rim of the pie dish. Brush with a little more water. Make a small cut in the centre of the remaining pastry and then lay it over the pie so that the pie funnel pokes through the cut. Press it on to the rim of the dish and crimp the edge with your fingers. Brush the top with beaten egg and decorate with leaves cut from the pastry trimmings. Bake in the oven for 35–40 minutes, until the pastry is crisp and golden.

smoked haddock kedgeree

There's a hint of Indian spice in my kedgeree; not enough to put you off your breakfast but just enough to serve as a faint reminder of where this dish came from.

SERVES 4

25 G (1 OZ) BUTTER

1 SMALL ONION, CHOPPED

2 GREEN CARDAMOM PODS, SPLIT OPEN

¼ TEASPOON TURMERIC POWDER

2.5 CM (1 IN) PIECE OF CINNAMON STICK

1 BAY LEAF, VERY FINELY SHREDDED

350 G (12 OZ) BASMATI RICE

600 ML (1 PINT) *CHICKEN STOCK* (SEE P. 140)

2 EGGS

450 G (1 LB) UNDYED SMOKED HADDOCK FILLET

2 TABLESPOONS CHOPPED FLAT-LEAF PARSLEY, PLUS A FEW SPRIGS
   TO GARNISH

SALT AND FRESHLY GROUND BLACK PEPPER

METHOD

Melt the butter in a large pan, add the onion and cook over a medium heat for 5 minutes, until soft but not browned. Add the cardamom pods, turmeric, cinnamon stick and shredded bay leaf and cook, stirring, for 1 minute.

Add the rice and stir for about 1 minute, until it is well coated in the spicy butter. Add the stock and ½ teaspoon of salt and bring to the boil. Cover the pan with a close-fitting lid, lower the heat and leave it to cook very gently for 15 minutes.

Meanwhile, hard-boil the eggs for 8 minutes. Bring some water to the boil in a large shallow pan, add the smoked haddock and simmer for 4 minutes, until the fish is just cooked. Lift the fish out on to a plate and leave until cool enough to handle, then break it into flakes, discarding the skin and any bones. Drain the eggs, cool slightly, then peel and cut into small pieces.

Uncover the rice and gently fork in the fish and the eggs. Cover again and return to the heat for 5 minutes or until the fish has heated through. Then gently stir in the chopped parsley and season with a little more salt and pepper to taste. Serve garnished with sprigs of parsley.

2 sole, plaice & tuna dishes

goujons of lemon sole with tartare sauce ■ **fillets of lemon sole** with a vermouth sauce and wholegrain mustard ■ **malaysian fried lemon sole** ■ **fillets of lemon sole** with ciabatta breadcrumbs and salsa verde mayonnaise ■ **grilled lemon sole** with lemongrass butter ■ **filets de sole joinville** ■ **classic sole normande** ■ **grilled lemon sole** with a roasted red pepper butter ■ **rui's turmeric fish** with masala dhal ■ **plaice with leeks**, mint and beaujolais ■ **fillets of plaice** with pancetta and beurre noisette ■ **grilled scored plaice** with roasted red pepper, garlic and oregano ■ **a salad of plaice** with ginger, lime and chilli ■ **a meurette of plaice** and lemon sole with beaujolais ■ **lemongrass plaice** with coriander salsa and coconut rice ■ **chargrilled tuna** with olives, lemon and sorrel ■ **chargrilled tuna** with salsa verde ■ **grilled tuna** with roasted fennel and tomatoes and apple balsamic vinegar ■ **grilled tuna salad** with guacamole ■ **grillade of tuna** with olive oil mash ■ **seared tuna** with rice noodles and coriander salad ■ **tonno con fagioli**

goujons of lemon sole with
tartare sauce

Goujons are small pieces of fish fillet, coated in breadcrumbs then deep-fried. We use a Japanese breadcrumb called *panko*: they fry much crisper than any other coating. They can, however, be hard to get hold of in shops or supermarkets so, if you do have trouble, use ordinary fresh breadcrumbs – you will still get perfectly acceptable results. These goujons make a perfect first course and are universally popular.

SERVES 4

350 G (12 OZ) LEMON SOLE FILLET, SKINNED (SEE P. 7)

25 G (1 OZ) PLAIN FLOUR, SEASONED WITH SALT AND PEPPER

2 EGGS

50 G (2 OZ) *PANKO* OR FRESH WHITE BREADCRUMBS

SUNFLOWER OIL, FOR DEEP-FRYING

1 LEMON

1 QUANTITY *TARTARE SAUCE* (SEE P. 141)

METHOD

To cut the lemon sole into goujons, slice the fillet diagonally to make long pieces about the size of your little finger. Put the seasoned flour in a small shallow dish or tray. Beat the eggs together and put in a second dish or tray and put the breadcrumbs in a third. Set the deep-fryer to 190°C/375°F, or heat some oil in a large pan to the same temperature or until a small piece of white bread dropped into the oil browns and rises to the surface in 1 minute.

Dip the goujons first in the seasoned flour, then the egg and finally the breadcrumbs and deep-fry until golden brown. Drain on kitchen paper and serve with the lemon, cut into wedges, and the tartare sauce.

fillets of lemon sole with a vermouth sauce and wholegrain mustard

The fillets of lemon sole are accompanied by a variation of the classic sauce *beurre blanc* (made with dry vermouth instead of white wine) and thinly sliced cucumber flavoured with Thai fish sauce (*nam pla*), which I use as a subtly flavoured substitute for salt, so if you can't get it use plain salt instead.

SERVES 4

½ CUCUMBER

12 x 65 G (2½ OZ) UNSKINNED LEMON SOLE FILLETS

MELTED BUTTER, FOR BRUSHING

1 TABLESPOON THAI FISH SAUCE (*NAM PLA*)

1 TEASPOON ROUGHLY CHOPPED CORIANDER

SALT AND FRESHLY GROUND WHITE PEPPER

FOR THE VERMOUTH SAUCE:

50 G (2 OZ) SHALLOTS OR ONIONS, FINELY CHOPPED

2 TABLESPOONS WHITE WINE VINEGAR

50 ML (2 FL OZ) DRY VERMOUTH

6 TABLESPOONS *FISH STOCK* (SEE P. 140) OR WATER

2 TABLESPOONS DOUBLE CREAM

175 G (6 OZ) UNSALTED BUTTER, CUT INTO PIECES

1 TEASPOON WHOLEGRAIN MUSTARD

METHOD

First prepare the cucumber by cutting it into sections about 5 cm (2 in) long, then slicing these into matchsticks.

For the vermouth sauce, put the shallots or onions, vinegar, vermouth and fish stock or water into a small pan, bring to the boil and simmer until nearly all the liquid has evaporated. Add the cream and reduce a little more, then remove the pan from the heat and whisk in the butter a little at a time until it has all amalgamated.

Pass the sauce through a sieve into a clean pan. Add the wholegrain mustard and a small pinch of salt. Keep warm.

Pre-heat the grill to high. Brush the fillets with butter, then season with salt and pepper. Cook under the grill for 4 minutes.

Put the cucumber in a small pan and add the fish sauce (or a good pinch of salt) and the coriander. Cover and cook gently for 2 minutes. Stir, then divide between 4 warmed plates. Arrange the lemon sole fillets neatly beside the cucumber so they overlap each other on the plates and pour the vermouth sauce all around. Serve immediately.

malaysian fried lemon sole

Here, lemon sole is dipped in a sauce made with red chilli, garlic, ginger and turmeric, then dusted with cornflour and deep-fried. It is a simple and delightfully spicy way of serving up any fillets of flat fish, such as plaice, dab or flounder, and can be accompanied by a simple green salad and maybe some plain rice.

SERVES 4

SUNFLOWER OIL, FOR DEEP-FRYING

175 G (6 OZ) CORNFLOUR

3 x 450 G (1 LB) LEMON SOLE, FILLETED AND SKINNED (SEE P. 7)

SALT AND FRESHLY GROUND BLACK PEPPER

FOR THE CHILLI SAUCE:

6 RED FINGER CHILLIES, ROUGHLY CHOPPED

4 GARLIC CLOVES, ROUGHLY CHOPPED

1 TEASPOON TURMERIC POWDER

5 CM (2 IN) FRESH ROOT GINGER, ROUGHLY CHOPPED

4 TABLESPOONS SUNFLOWER OIL

1 TEASPOON SALT

2 TABLESPOONS VINEGAR

4-6 TABLESPOONS COLD WATER

METHOD

For the chilli sauce, put all the ingredients into a liquidizer and blend until smooth. Pour into a pan and simmer gently for 10 minutes or so until the mixture begins to separate.

Pour the sunflower oil into a large pan until it is about a third full. Heat to 190°C/375°F or until a small piece of white bread dropped into the oil browns and rises to the surface in 1 minute. Put the chilli sauce in one shallow dish and the cornflour in another. Season the fish fillets with salt and pepper and dip them first into the chilli sauce and then into the cornflour, making sure that it coats the fish evenly. Cook 2 or 3 fillets in the hot oil for about 2 minutes or until crisp and golden. Lift out with a slotted spoon and drain on kitchen paper. Keep warm while you cook the rest.

fillets of lemon sole with ciabatta
breadcrumbs and salsa verde mayonnaise

Of all fish, lemon sole is best suited to deep-frying in breadcrumbs. The only other way of eating it is cooked on the bone, as in the recipe for *Grilled Lemon Sole with Lemongrass Butter* on p. 48. I love salsa verde and thought a little of it folded into some mayonnaise would go very well with lemon sole fillets coated in breadcrumbs made with Italian ciabatta, preferably one with black olives. It's now a dish that features on the Seafood Restaurant menu five times a week. When you start to eat this, served with a bowl of crisp chips, a salad sparingly dressed with perfect extra virgin olive oil and a glass of crisp Italian wine like Vernaccia di San Gimignano, well, you feel jolly full of beans.

SERVES 4

SUNFLOWER OIL, FOR DEEP-FRYING

1 LOAF OF BLACK OLIVE CIABATTA

12 x 65 G (2½ OZ) LEMON SOLE FILLETS, SKINNED (SEE P. 7)

50 G (2 OZ) PLAIN FLOUR

2 LARGE EGGS, BEATEN

SALT AND FRESHLY GROUND BLACK PEPPER

LEMON WEDGES

FOR THE SALSA VERDE MAYONNAISE:

3 HEAPED TABLESPOONS PARSLEY LEAVES

1 HEAPED TABLESPOON MINT LEAVES

3 TABLESPOONS CAPERS, DRAINED

6 ANCHOVY FILLETS IN OIL, DRAINED

1 GARLIC CLOVE

6 TABLESPOONS *MAYONNAISE* (SEE P. 141) MADE WITH OLIVE OIL

1 TEASPOON DIJON MUSTARD

1 TABLESPOON LEMON JUICE

½ TEASPOON SALT

METHOD

For the salsa verde mayonnaise, coarsely chop the parsley, mint, capers, anchovy fillets and garlic all together and mix with the mayonnaise, mustard, lemon juice and salt.

Heat some oil for deep-frying to 190°C/375°F or until a small piece of white bread dropped into the oil browns and rises to the surface in 1 minute. Turn the ciabatta into fine breadcrumbs. Season the fish fillets with a little salt and pepper, then coat each one with flour, then beaten egg, then breadcrumbs.

Deep-fry 2 pieces for about 2 minutes, until crisp and golden. Drain on kitchen paper and keep warm while you fry the rest. Serve straight away with the salsa verde mayonnaise, some lemon wedges and a leafy salad.

grilled lemon sole with lemongrass butter

Here's a paean to lemon sole. Several years ago I was asked to meet some buyers from Tesco's supermarket at Plymouth fish market, to look at the quality of the fish there. They were exploring an idea about supplementing the centrally bought fish from Grimsby, sold at their fish counters, with good local fish in season; an idea which has now become reality. It was early March when we visited the market – during a spell of spring high pressure, calm seas and good fishing. There was a lot of fish, all caught-that-day fresh: red mullet glistening pink with flashes of yellow and eyes so clear you could gaze to the bottom of the sea through them; and lemon sole, bright of eye and stiff and slimy. I felt so proud of our local fish. You wouldn't see better in a market anywhere in the world. I can think of no better way to cook beautifully fresh lemon sole than by simply grilling it. Here it's served with a typically British flavoured butter, but I've added a modern spin to it with a few Thai ingredients.

SERVES 4

4 x 350–450 G (12 OZ–1 LB) UNSKINNED LEMON SOLE

15 G (½ OZ) BUTTER, MELTED

SALT AND FRESHLY GROUND BLACK PEPPER

FOR THE LEMONGRASS BUTTER:

1 LEMONGRASS STALK, OUTER LEAVES REMOVED AND THE CORE
   VERY FINELY CHOPPED

FINELY GRATED ZEST OF ½ LIME

2 TEASPOONS LIME JUICE

1 CM (½ IN) FRESH ROOT GINGER, VERY FINELY CHOPPED

2 TABLESPOONS CHOPPED PARSLEY

100 G (4 OZ) SLIGHTLY SALTED BUTTER, SOFTENED

1 TABLESPOON THAI FISH SAUCE (*NAM PLA*)

METHOD

First make the lemongrass butter. Put everything into a food processor and season well with pepper. Blend until smooth, then spoon the mixture into the centre of a large sheet of cling film, shape into a roll 4 cm (1½ in) thick, wrap and chill in the fridge or freezer until firm.

When the butter is firm, pre-heat the grill to high. Prepare the fish by cutting off the frills plus about 1 cm (½ in) of flesh with kitchen scissors to remove all the lateral bones. Then trim down the tails and trim off all the other little fins. Brush the fish on both sides with the melted butter and season with a little salt and pepper. Depending on the size of your grill, cook 1 or 2, dark-side up, on a buttered baking tray or the rack of a grill pan, for 7–8 minutes or until the flesh is firm and white at the thickest part, just behind the head. Keep warm while you cook the rest.

Unwrap the lemongrass butter and slice into thin rounds and serve on top of the fish.

GRILLED LEMON SOLE WITH LEMONGRASS BUTTER · SOLE, PLAICE & TUNA DISHES   49

filets de sole joinville

This is a classic sautéed dish from the Normandy town of Joinville. It would once have been made with Dover sole fillets but I am loath to do anything with Dover sole other than cook it whole, grilled or *à la meunière* – the latter being the whole fish cooked just as in this recipe but without the mushrooms and shrimps.

Lemon sole is very easy to buy ready-filleted and has a really good flavour. The only slight drawback is that it tends to be a bit delicate and therefore you need to be careful when turning the fillets during cooking. Ideally this starter should be made with those little brown shrimps but I have also given the right quantity of North Atlantic prawns bought in the shell, which are so much better-flavoured than those prepared ones that you get in sandwiches.

SERVES 4

8 LARGE UNSKINNED LEMON SOLE FILLETS

50 G (2 OZ) PLAIN FLOUR, WELL SEASONED WITH SALT AND PEPPER

50 G (2 OZ) *CLARIFIED BUTTER* (SEE P. 142)

225 G (8 OZ) SMALL BUTTON MUSHROOMS, THINLY SLICED

75 G (3 OZ) COOKED PEELED BROWN SHRIMPS OR 24 COOKED PEELED
    NORTH ATLANTIC PRAWNS

100 G (4 OZ) UNSALTED BUTTER

JUICE OF 1 LEMON

3 TABLESPOONS CHOPPED PARSLEY

SALT AND FRESHLY GROUND WHITE PEPPER

METHOD

Season the lemon sole fillets on both sides with a little salt and pepper. Dip them in the seasoned flour so that they are well coated on both sides, then dust off the excess.

Heat the clarified butter in a heavy-based frying pan and fry the fish fillets in a couple of batches for 1 minute on each side. Add the mushrooms and fry, then add the shrimps or prawns at the last minute just to warm through. Arrange the fish fillets, mushrooms and shrimps on a warm serving plate.

Wipe out the pan and heat the butter until it begins to brown and smell nutty. Add the lemon juice, parsley and a good pinch of salt and pour over the fish. Serve with sautéed potatoes and a green lettuce salad.

classic sole normande

There are hundreds of recipes for whole lemon sole poached with a little cider, fish stock and flavouring ingredients but this, in my opinion, is the best. Whole flat fish have lots of tiny little bones that run along the sides of them, but in this recipe, all those bones are simply removed after cooking, making the fish easy to eat. Serve with boiled new potatoes.

SERVES 4

4 x 300–350 G (10–12 OZ) LEMON SOLE

24 UNSHELLED NORTH ATLANTIC PRAWNS

450 ML (15 FL OZ) *FISH STOCK* (SEE P. 140)

350 G (12 OZ) MUSSELS, CLEANED (SEE P. 7)

2 SHALLOTS, VERY THINLY SLICED

175 G (6 OZ) BUTTON MUSHROOMS, THINLY SLICED

85 ML (3 FL OZ) DRY CIDER (NORMANDY IF POSSIBLE)

25 G (1 OZ) BUTTER, SOFTENED

20 G (¾ OZ) PLAIN FLOUR

2 EGG YOLKS

150 ML (5 FL OZ) DOUBLE CREAM

1 TABLESPOON CHOPPED PARSLEY

SALT AND FRESHLY GROUND BLACK PEPPER

METHOD

Pre-heat the oven to 190°C/375°F/Gas 5. Trim the fins off the lemon sole using kitchen scissors and peel all but 8 of the prawns.

Place the fish stock in a pan and bring to the boil. Add the mussels, cover and cook over a high heat for 3–4 minutes, until the mussels have opened. Discard any that remain closed. Tip them into a sieve set over a bowl. Reserve the stock. Remove the meats from all but 8 of the mussel shells.

Sprinkle the shallots and mushrooms over the base of a shallow ovenproof dish or roasting tin large enough to take the fish side by side in 1 layer (they can overlap very slightly if need be). Place the fish on top and season. Pour over all but the last tablespoon of stock (this might contain a little sand from the mussels) and then the cider. Cover with foil and bake for 15 minutes.

Lift the fish on to a board. Remove the side bones by dragging them out with the blade of a sharp knife – they will pull out quite easily. Transfer the fish to 4 warmed plates, garnish with the mussels in their shells and the unpeeled prawns and set aside. Pre-heat the grill to its highest setting.

Melt the butter in a pan. Stir in the flour and cook for 30 seconds. Take the pan off the heat and gradually stir in the cooking juices and vegetables from the baking dish. Bring to the boil, stirring, and simmer for 10–15 minutes.

Mix the egg yolks with the cream, stir into the sauce and simmer for 1–2 minutes until it coats the back of a spoon. Stir in the shelled prawns, mussels and parsley and season. Spoon the sauce over each fish and slide each one under the grill for 1–2 minutes until the sauce is lightly flecked with brown.

grilled lemon sole with a roasted red pepper butter

I'm very fond of lemon sole as it's not particularly expensive and, with its sweet flavour, is one of the best value fish on the market. I prefer lemon sole on the bone, especially if you cut off the little lateral bones in the frills on either side of the fish, before cooking.

SERVES 4

4 x 350–450 G (12 OZ–1 LB) UNSKINNED LEMON SOLE

15 G (½ OZ) BUTTER, MELTED

SALT AND FRESHLY GROUND BLACK PEPPER

LEMON WEDGES

FOR THE FLAVOURED BUTTER:

1 SMALL RED PEPPER, HALVED LENGTHWAYS AND SEEDED

2 SUN-DRIED TOMATOES IN OLIVE OIL, DRAINED

1 MEDIUM-HOT RED FINGER CHILLI SUCH AS CAYENNE OR
   DUTCH CHILLI, SEEDED

100 G (4 OZ) SLIGHTLY SALTED BUTTER, SOFTENED

2 TABLESPOONS CHOPPED PARSLEY

METHOD

First make the flavoured butter. Pre-heat the oven to 220°C/425°F/Gas 7. Roast the red pepper for 20–25 minutes, turning once until the skin is black. Then remove the pepper from the heat and leave to cool. Break it in half and remove the stalk, skin and seeds.

Finely chop the red pepper, the sun-dried tomatoes and the red chilli and mix into the softened butter with the parsley and ½ teaspoon of salt. Spoon the mixture into the centre of a large sheet of cling film and shape into a roll about 4 cm (1½ in) thick. Wrap and chill in the fridge or freezer until firm.

Pre-heat the grill to high. Prepare the fish by cutting off the frills plus about 1 cm (½ in) of flesh with kitchen scissors to remove all the lateral bones. Then trim down the tails and trim off all the other little fins.

Brush the fish on both sides with some melted butter and season with a little salt and pepper. Depending on the size of your grill, cook 1 or 2, dark-side up and on 1 side only, on a buttered baking tray or the rack of the grill pan for 7–8 minutes. To tell whether the fish is done, part the flesh at its thickest point just behind the head – it should be firm and opaque close to the bone. If it's not quite done, cook it for about 1 minute more, but don't be tempted to try to turn it over or it might fall apart. Keep it warm while you cook the rest.

Unwrap the red pepper butter and slice it into thin rounds. Lift the fish, dark-side up, on to heatproof plates and place 3–4 rounds of the butter along the back of each fish. Flash back under the grill very briefly until the butter just begins to melt, then serve with lemon wedges.

rui's turmeric fish with masala dhal

My friend Rui, from Goa, cooked this dish for Jill and me and our sons when he came to Cornwall. We went wild about it but Rui, who is very modest, couldn't understand what all the fuss was about – he said that he'd just cooked it up from the spices he'd found in the kitchen cupboards. But no one in England would have done it quite like this. So we asked him to cook it once more when we filmed in Goa, in the back garden of a beautiful old blue-and-white Portuguese house. I was worried that he might lose it a bit in front of the camera but he was a natural and the dish was as good then as it was back in Padstow. Rui stirs some quickly fried mustard seeds, ginger, onions, tomatoes and green chilli into the dhal right at the end of cooking. Now that's real fun.

SERVES 4

1 TEASPOON SALT

JUICE OF 1 LIME

1 TEASPOON TURMERIC POWDER

4 x 175-225 G (6-8 OZ) THICK LEMON SOLE FILLETS, SKINNED (SEE P. 7)

3 TABLESPOONS VEGETABLE OIL

FOR THE MASALA DHAL:

250 G (9 OZ) RED LENTILS

225 G (8 OZ) ONIONS

225 G (8 OZ) TOMATOES

175 G (6 OZ) GHEE OR *CLARIFIED BUTTER* (SEE P. 142)

2 GARLIC CLOVES, FINELY CHOPPED

1 TABLESPOON TURMERIC POWDER

1 TEASPOON CHILLI POWDER

150 ML (5 FL OZ) COCONUT MILK

15 G (½ OZ) BLACK MUSTARD SEEDS

2.5 CM (1 IN) FRESH ROOT GINGER, FINELY CHOPPED

2 GREEN FINGER CHILLIES, SEEDED AND FINELY CHOPPED

A PINCH OF ASAFOETIDA (OPTIONAL)

3 TABLESPOONS ROUGHLY CHOPPED CORIANDER

SALT

METHOD

For the dhal, cover the lentils with 600 ml (1 pint) of water and leave them to soak. Coarsely chop half the onions and finely chop the rest. Cut half the tomatoes into small chunks and finely dice the rest. Heat half the ghee or clarified butter in a heavy-based pan. Fry the garlic, coarsely chopped onions and tomato chunks for 5 minutes, until the mixture has cooked to a golden-brown paste. Pour in the lentils and their soaking water and bring to the boil. Add the turmeric, chilli powder and coconut milk and simmer until the lentils have broken down and the mixture has thickened (about 30 minutes). Season to taste with some salt and remove from the heat.

   To finish the dhal, heat the rest of the ghee or clarified butter in a large, deep frying pan. Add the mustard seeds, cover the pan with a lid and fry until the seeds begin to pop. Add the ginger, the rest of the onions and tomatoes, the chillies and the asafoetida, if using. Cook for 5 minutes and then pour everything into the lentil mixture and stir well. Keep warm while you fry the fish.

Mix the salt, lime juice and turmeric together and rub well into the fish fillets. Heat the oil in a large, non-stick frying pan, add the fillets and fry for 2–3 minutes on each side. Stir the coriander into the dhal and serve with the fish. This would be great served with kachumber salad (see p. 140).

plaice with leeks, mint and beaujolais

This is one of the most successful dishes for plaice – we've had it on the menu in my restaurant for years. I think its success lies in the almost indefinable satisfaction of the three components – the watery fragrance of the plaice, the tartness of the Beaujolais sauce and the freshness of mint with the leeks, with the slight taste of smoke from the bacon.

SERVES 4

1 x 100 G (4 OZ) LEEK, CLEANED

100 G (4 OZ) BUTTER

1 RASHER OF RINDLESS SMOKED BACK BACON, CUT INTO THIN STRIPS

1 TEASPOON CHOPPED MINT

175 ML (6 FL OZ) BEAUJOLAIS

50 ML (2 FL OZ) PORT

300 ML (10 FL OZ) *FISH STOCK* (SEE P. 140)

¼ TEASPOON CASTER SUGAR

4 x 75 G (3 OZ) PLAICE FILLETS, SKINNED (SEE P. 7)

SALT AND FRESHLY GROUND WHITE PEPPER

SPRIGS OF MINT, TO GARNISH

METHOD

Cut the leek in half lengthways and once more into quarters. Cut across these strips into 1 cm (½ in) pieces. Bring a small pan of salted water to the boil, add the leek and simmer for a few minutes until tender but still *al dente*. Drain well.

Melt 15 g (½ oz) of the butter in a small pan, add the bacon and leek and cook gently until all the excess water has evaporated. Stir in the chopped mint and season with some salt and pepper. Set aside and keep warm.

Pre-heat the grill to high. Put the Beaujolais, port, fish stock and sugar into a large pan and boil rapidly until reduced by three-quarters.

Melt another 15 g (½ oz) of the butter and brush over both sides of each plaice fillet. Season with salt and pepper and lay them on the lightly oiled rack of the grill pan. Grill for 2 minutes.

Dice the remaining butter. Bring the reduced wine and stock back up to the boil and then whisk in the butter, a few small pieces at a time. Adjust the seasoning if necessary.

To serve, spoon the leeks on to 4 warmed plates. Put the plaice fillets on top and pour the sauce around. Garnish with sprigs of mint.

fillets of plaice with pancetta and beurre noisette

This incredibly simple dish relies on presentation for its effect. The fillets of fish are arranged down the centre of a nice oval serving dish, interleaved with thin slices of fried pancetta or, if you can't get it, extremely thinly sliced bacon. It looks wonderful when surrounded with *beurre noisette*, which is simply butter heated until brown and nutty-smelling, then sharpened with lemon juice. Next time you're in France and wandering through a market, do make sure you buy one of those long, narrow, elegant, white oval fish dishes for presenting food like this. Owing to the demise of silver service in restaurants, it is all too rare to see dishes served up in a formal manner from the kitchen but if it's done well it is extremely effective. I suspect that, as everything in restaurant cooking appears to be of a cyclical nature, the era of presenting beautiful large platters of food at the table will return.

SERVES 4

16 SMALL, VERY THIN SLICES OF SMOKED PANCETTA (OR 8 THIN RASHERS
   OF RINDLESS SMOKED STREAKY BACON, HALVED)
2 TABLESPOONS SUNFLOWER OIL
40 G (1½ OZ) UNSALTED BUTTER
25 G (1 OZ) PLAIN FLOUR
½ TEASPOON SALT
10 TURNS OF THE WHITE PEPPER MILL
8 x 75–100 G (3-4 OZ) PLAICE FILLETS, SKINNED (SEE P. 7)
JUICE OF ¼ LEMON
2 TEASPOONS CHOPPED FRESH *FINES HERBES* (PARSLEY, CHERVIL,
   CHIVES AND TARRAGON)

METHOD

Pre-heat the grill to high. Grill the slices of pancetta or streaky bacon for 1–1½ minutes on each side, until crisp. Set aside and keep warm.

Heat the oil and 15 g (½ oz) of the butter in a large frying pan. Season the flour with the salt and pepper and spread it over a large plate. Cut each plaice fillet across in half and then dip the pieces in the seasoned flour. Fry for 2 minutes on each side, until lightly golden, then arrange them down the centre of a warmed oval serving platter, interleaving them with the slices of grilled pancetta or bacon.

Discard the frying oil and add the remaining butter and allow it to melt over a moderate heat. When the butter starts to smell nutty and turn light brown, quickly add the lemon juice and herbs and then pour it right over the fish and bacon. Serve straight away.

grilled scored plaice with roasted
red pepper, garlic and oregano

The fish, scored and marinated with olive oil, garlic, oregano, chilli and sea salt, is good served with a bowl of chips and a soft lettuce salad with mustard and chive dressing. I have never forgotten the wonderful earthy flavour of some chips eaten in a taverna in Paxos, Greece, caused by not being too fastidious with the peeling. Just roughly peel some potatoes (such as Maris Piper) leaving on some of the peel, then cut into large, irregular chips and deep-fry in hot oil.

SERVES 4

4 x 450 G (1 LB) UNSKINNED PLAICE

1 RED PEPPER

½ MEDIUM-HOT RED DUTCH CHILLI, SEEDED AND FINELY CHOPPED

50 ML (2 FL OZ) EXTRA VIRGIN OLIVE OIL

1 LARGE GARLIC CLOVE, FINELY CHOPPED

1 TEASPOON CHOPPED OREGANO

2 TEASPOONS LEMON JUICE

1 TEASPOON SALT

FRESHLY GROUND BLACK PEPPER

METHOD

Prepare the fish by cutting off the frills plus about 1 cm (½ in) of flesh with kitchen scissors to remove all the lateral bones. Then trim down the tails and trim off all the other little fins. Put the fish, dark-side up, on a board. Make a deep cut down the centre of each fish from head to tail. Then make a series of smaller cuts out from the first one towards the sides so that they look like the veins of a leaf. Turn the fish over and repeat on the other side.

Roast the red pepper by placing it in an oven pre-heated to 220°C/425 °F/ Gas 7 for 20–25 minutes, turning once until the skin is black. Then remove the pepper from the heat and leave to cool. Break it in half and remove the stalk, skin and seeds. Chop the flesh finely and mix with the chilli, oil, garlic, oregano, lemon juice, salt and some pepper to make the marinade.

One hour before cooking, put the fish into a shallow dish and pour over the marinade, making sure it goes right into the slashes. Set aside.

Pre-heat the grill to high. Transfer the fish to baking trays, dark-side up. Depending on the size of your grill, cook 1 or 2 fish at a time for 7–8 minutes or until the flesh is firm and white at the thickest part, just behind the head. Spoon over some of the remaining marinade 4 minutes before the end of cooking. Keep warm while you cook the rest. Serve with some chips and a salad of soft green leaves.

a salad of plaice with ginger, lime and chilli

This ceviche of plaice is perfectly off-set, I think, by a line of wafer-thin slices of beef tomatoes dressed with a little extra virgin olive oil and salt.

SERVES 4

350 G (12 OZ) PLAICE FILLETS, SKINNED (SEE P. 7)

2 LIMES

1 CM (½ IN) FRESH ROOT GINGER, PEELED AND VERY FINELY CHOPPED

2 RED BIRD'S EYE CHILLIES, SEEDED AND VERY FINELY CHOPPED

1 TABLESPOON CHOPPED CORIANDER

2 SMALL BEEFSTEAK TOMATOES, VERY THINLY SLICED

EXTRA VIRGIN OLIVE OIL

SALT

SPRIGS OF CORIANDER, TO GARNISH

METHOD

Cut the plaice fillets into long thin strips about the thickness of your little finger, then place in a shallow non-metallic dish.

Coarsely grate the rind from half of 1 lime, then squeeze the juices from both. Pour over the fish and add the ginger, chillies, chopped coriander and 1 teaspoon of salt. Mix well, cover and chill for 3 hours.

Spoon the plaice on to one side of each of 4 plates. Arrange a line of overlapping tomato slices on the other side, then sprinkle them with a little olive oil and 1 teaspoon of salt and garnish with sprigs of coriander.

a meurette of plaice and lemon sole with beaujolais

This Burgundian freshwater fish stew calls for plenty of fruity red wine to produce a robust, full-flavoured dish.

SERVES 4

350 G (12 OZ) UNSKINNED PLAICE FILLETS

350 G (12 OZ) UNSKINNED LEMON SOLE FILLETS

25 G (1 OZ) UNSALTED BUTTER MIXED WITH 15 G (½ OZ) FLOUR (*BEURRE MANIÉ*)

SALT AND FRESHLY GROUND BLACK PEPPER

FOR THE CROÛTONS:

2 SLICES OF WHITE BREAD

25 ML (1 FL OZ) GROUNDNUT OIL

A KNOB OF BUTTER

FOR THE RED WINE STOCK:

25 G (1 OZ) BUTTER

225 G (8 OZ) EQUAL QUANTITIES OF CARROT, CELERY, LEEK AND ONION,
  CHOPPED AND MIXED TOGETHER

1 TABLESPOON BRANDY

1.2 LITRES (2 PINTS) *CHICKEN STOCK* (SEE P. 140)

½ BOTTLE BEAUJOLAIS

1 BAY LEAF

A SPRIG OF THYME OR ½ TEASPOON DRIED THYME

FOR THE *MEURETTE*:

24 SHALLOTS, PEELED

¼ TEASPOON SUGAR

15 G (½ OZ) BUTTER

FOR THE MUSHROOM AND BACON GARNISH:

1 RASHER RINDLESS SMOKED BACK BACON, CUT INTO THIN STRIPS

15 G (½ OZ) BUTTER

225 G (8 OZ) BUTTON MUSHROOMS, CUT INTO QUARTERS

FOR THE PERSILLADE:

1 SMALL GARLIC CLOVE

A SMALL BUNCH OF PARSLEY

METHOD

First make the croûtons. Using a 2.5 cm (1 in) round cutter, cut out 8 discs from the slices of bread and fry them in the groundnut oil, adding a little knob of butter to the pan to give them a golden colour.

For the red wine stock, melt the butter in a pan and add the chopped mixed vegetables (known as *mirepoix*) and fry them until they are just beginning to brown. Add the brandy and boil off the alcohol before adding 900 ml (1½ pints) of the chicken stock, and the Beaujolais, bay leaf and thyme. Bring to the boil and simmer for 30 minutes.

Meanwhile, for the *meurette*, brown the shallots with the sugar and butter in a shallow pan. Add the remaining chicken stock and simmer the shallots gently until they are tender, then turn up the heat and reduce the shallots and stock until you have a shiny brown glaze. Set aside and keep warm.

For the garnish, fry the bacon gently in the butter, then add the mushrooms and continue to fry until soft. Season then set aside and keep warm.

Finely chop the garlic and parsley together to make the *persillade*.

Strain the red wine stock into a shallow pan, bring to the boil and boil rapidly to reduce the volume by half. Add the fish fillets and cook gently until just tender. (This should take about 5 minutes.)

Remove the fillets from the pan and place neatly on a warmed serving dish. Break the *beurre manié* into small pieces and stir into the red wine sauce. Continue to stir until the sauce thickens. Add the *meurette*, the mushroom and bacon garnish and the *persillade*. Check the seasoning and add a little salt, if necessary. Spoon the sauce over the fish, top with the croûtons and serve.

lemongrass plaice with coriander salsa and coconut rice

Coconut rice is a must. I've taken fillets of rather underwhelmingly flavoured plaice, coated them with a delicate green lemongrass, chilli and coriander paste, then grilled them to serve with the rice and a slightly sweet salsa. This dish suggests some of the lighter cooking from areas like Kuala Lumpur and Singapore, which are reflected in Australian cuisine. We in the West tend to think of those places as having traditional time-honoured dishes yet, in fact, they are just as likely to experiment with quick cooking techniques and light flavours as we are.

SERVES 4

12 x 50 G (2 OZ) PLAICE FILLETS, SKINNED (SEE P. 7)

FOR THE LEMONGRASS AND CHILLI PASTE:
5 LEMONGRASS STALKS, OUTER LEAVES REMOVED AND THE CORES
    ROUGHLY CHOPPED
6 RED BIRD'S EYE CHILLIES, ROUGHLY CHOPPED
6 GARLIC CLOVES, ROUGHLY CHOPPED
3 KAFFIR LIME LEAVES OR STRIPS OF LIME ZEST
A SMALL BUNCH OF CORIANDER
120 ML (4 FL OZ) SUNFLOWER OIL
1½ TABLESPOONS THAI FISH SAUCE (*NAM PLA*)
1½ TEASPOONS FRESHLY GROUND BLACK PEPPER

FOR THE COCONUT RICE:
1 TABLESPOON *CLARIFIED BUTTER* (SEE P. 142)
175 G (6 OZ) THAI JASMINE RICE
300 ML (10 FL OZ) COCONUT MILK
½ TEASPOON SALT
1 SMALL BAY LEAF

FOR THE TOMATO AND CORIANDER SALSA:
2 TOMATOES, CUT INTO SMALL DICE
2 SPRING ONIONS, SLICED
1 TABLESPOON RED WINE VINEGAR
A PINCH OF CASTER SUGAR
A PINCH OF CAYENNE PEPPER
A PINCH OF SALT
2 TABLESPOONS CHOPPED CORIANDER

METHOD

First make the lemongrass and chilli paste: put all the ingredients into a food processor and blend until smooth.

For the coconut rice, heat the clarified butter in a pan, add the rice and stir around until all the grains are coated in the butter. Add all but 2 tablespoons of the coconut milk, plus 50 ml (2 fl oz) of water and the salt and bay leaf. Bring to the boil, cover and reduce the heat to low. Cook for 15 minutes, until all the liquid has been absorbed and the rice is tender.

Meanwhile, mix together all the ingredients for the salsa and set to one side.

Pre-heat the grill to high. Mix the lemongrass and chilli paste with the reserved coconut milk. Lay the plaice fillets on a lightly oiled baking tray and brush each one with some of the mixture, then grill the fish for 3 minutes. Serve with the coconut rice and salsa.

chargrilled tuna with olives, lemon and sorrel

This recipe comes from Gay Bilson, an inspired cook from Sydney. Her restaurant, The Berowra Waters Inn, produced one of the most memorable meals of my life. She has now moved on to running a restaurant in the Opera House. The tuna fish fillet is seared on the outside but left underdone inside; this is by far the best way to eat it. A cast-iron ribbed steak pan is the ideal utensil for cooking this dish, though a real barbecue imparts a superior flavour. The quantities are for a first course.

SERVES 4

12 GREEN OLIVES

50 G (2 OZ) SORREL

450 G (1 LB) TUNA FILLET

50 ML (2 FL OZ) VIRGIN OLIVE OIL

½ TEASPOON THAI FISH SAUCE (*NAM PLA*)

JUICE OF ¼ LEMON

SALT AND FRESHLY GROUND BLACK PEPPER

METHOD

Remove the stones from the olives and cut into thin slivers. Wash the sorrel, remove the stalks and cut into long, fine strips.

Put the grill pan on the heat to get really hot. Cut the tuna fillet into 4 pieces and brush with a little of the olive oil and season well with salt and pepper. Grill for 1 minute only on each side.

Put the fish sauce, lemon juice, 2½ teaspoons of the olive oil and 25 ml (1 fl oz) of water into a small pan. Bring to the boil, then remove from the heat immediately and keep warm.

Warm the remaining olive oil in another small pan, add the olives and about three-quarters of the sorrel. Allow the sorrel to wilt but don't cook it any further or it will brown.

Divide the olive and sorrel sauce between 4 warmed plates, place the tuna on top and pour the other sauce over the fish. Sprinkle with the remaining sorrel and serve.

chargrilled tuna with salsa verde

I'm always amazed how quickly tuna cooks. It's because it has such an open texture and so the heat penetrates very quickly. The steaks in this recipe need literally just one minute on either side if your barbecue or ridged cast-iron griddle is at the correct temperature. This is a dish of classic simplicity: one of the best sauces in the world combined with one of the best fish for cooking on a barbecue. A perfect summer dish, served with either a mixture of baby vegetables or a bowl of chips and some salad.

SERVES 4

4 x 175-225 G (6-8 OZ) THICK TUNA LOIN STEAKS
A LITTLE OLIVE OIL
SALT AND FRESHLY GROUND BLACK PEPPER

FOR THE SALSA VERDE:
3 TABLESPOONS FLAT-LEAF PARSLEY LEAVES
1 TABLESPOON MINT LEAVES
3 TABLESPOONS CAPERS, DRAINED
6 ANCHOVY FILLETS IN OIL, DRAINED
1 GARLIC CLOVE
1 TEASPOON DIJON MUSTARD
JUICE OF ½ LEMON
120 ML (4 FL OZ) EXTRA VIRGIN OLIVE OIL
½ TEASPOON SALT

METHOD

You can make the salsa verde some time in advance. I like to hand-chop all the ingredients on a board so that the sauce has plenty of rugged texture. By all means use a food processor if you prefer but don't turn it on for too long. Chop the parsley, mint, capers, anchovy fillets and garlic together. Scoop them into a bowl and stir in the mustard, lemon juice, olive oil and ½ teaspoon of salt.

If you are going to cook the tuna on a barbecue, make sure that you light it a good 40 minutes before cooking the steaks. Brush them on both sides with some oil and season well with salt and pepper. If you are using a ridged cast-iron griddle, place it over a high heat and leave it to get smoking hot, then drizzle it with a little oil. Now cook the tuna steaks for 1 minute on either side until nicely striped from the griddle on both sides but still pink and juicy in the centre.

Put the tuna on 4 warmed plates and spoon some salsa verde on top. Serve with either vegetables or some roughly cut chips.

grilled tuna with roasted fennel and tomatoes and apple balsamic vinegar

I think the best restaurant in Noosa, Australia, at the time of writing is Season. It's just the sort of restaurant I like – simple but high-quality ingredients perfectly cooked without pretension. This dish was on the menu last time I was there but this is not their recipe, just my idea of how they might have done it. If you cannot get apple balsamic vinegar, use ordinary balsamic vinegar instead.

SERVES 4

2 BULBS OF FENNEL
450 G (1 LB) LARGE PLUM TOMATOES
OLIVE OIL
4 x 175-225 G (6-8 OZ) THICK TUNA LOIN STEAKS
SEA SALT FLAKES AND COARSELY CRUSHED BLACK PEPPERCORNS

FOR THE SAUCE:
1 TABLESPOON APPLE BALSAMIC VINEGAR
½ TEASPOON FENNEL SEEDS, LIGHTLY CRUSHED
½ TEASPOON BLACK PEPPERCORNS, COARSELY CRUSHED
85 ML (3 FL OZ) EXTRA VIRGIN OLIVE OIL
½ TEASPOON SEA SALT FLAKES

METHOD

Pre-heat the oven to 240°C/475°F/Gas 9. Cut each fennel bulb lengthways through the root into 5 thin slices so they stay together in one piece. Drop them into a pan of boiling water, bring back to the boil and cook for 1 minute. Drain on kitchen paper.

Remove the cores from the tomatoes, cut them in half and place, cut-side up, in a lightly oiled shallow roasting tin. Sprinkle over some salt and pepper. Lay the fennel slices on an oiled baking tray, sprinkle with a little oil and some salt and pepper. Roast the tomatoes and the fennel for 20 minutes, then remove the tray of fennel slices. Reduce the oven temperature to 150°C/300°F/Gas 2 and leave the tomatoes to roast for a further 1½ hours.

For the sauce, put the apple balsamic vinegar, fennel seeds, black pepper and olive oil into a small pan and set aside.

Shortly before the tomatoes have finished roasting, pre-heat the grill to high. Brush the tuna steaks on both sides with olive oil, season well with salt and pepper and place on the rack of the grill pan or on a baking tray. Grill for just 3 minutes on each side. Put the fennel back in the oven to heat through. Set the pan of sauce over a very low heat just to warm through.

To serve, put the roasted vegetables on 4 warmed plates. Put the tuna on top and sprinkle with some sea salt flakes and pepper. Stir the ½ teaspoon of sea salt flakes into the sauce and spoon it around the outside of each plate.

grilled tuna salad with guacamole

This dish comes from the Fifth Floor Restaurant in Harvey Nichols department store in London. The idea that raw tuna is cooked on a charcoal grill so briefly that only the outside is coloured and caramelized and the inside practically raw has been much copied. But I know from talking to the chef, Henry Harris, at the Fifth Floor, that he was the one that brought the dish to England from California. This is not his exact recipe. I much prefer to get enthusiastic about a dish in someone else's restaurant than attempt to copy it. By doing this, two surprisingly different versions of the same dish emerge; two for the price of one, if you like.

SERVES 4

450 G (1 LB) PIECE OF TUNA LOIN FILLET

SEA SALT AND FRESHLY GROUND BLACK PEPPER

4 SPRIGS OF CORIANDER, TO GARNISH

FOR THE GUACAMOLE:

1 LARGE AVOCADO

1 JALAPEÑO CHILLI, SEEDED

JUICE OF 1 LIME

2 SPRING ONIONS, CHOPPED

1 TABLESPOON CHOPPED CORIANDER

3 TABLESPOONS SUNFLOWER OIL

½ TEASPOON SALT

FOR THE SOY DRESSING:

50 ML (2 FL OZ) WATER

1 TABLESPOON DARK SOY SAUCE

1 SPRING ONION, FINELY CHOPPED

¼ JALAPEÑO OR GREEN DUTCH CHILLI, SEEDED AND CHOPPED

JUICE AND ZEST OF ½ LIME

½ LEMONGRASS STALK, OUTER LEAVES REMOVED AND THE CORE
   FINELY SLICED

1 TEASPOON FINELY CHOPPED FRESH GINGER

METHOD

Heat a ridged cast-iron griddle until it is very hot. Brush the piece of tuna with oil and sprinkle liberally with salt and pepper. Cook the tuna for 1–1½ minutes on each face, until coloured all over. Remember the centre of the tuna should remain raw. Remove from the pan and season again. Leave to cool completely.

For the guacamole, blend all the ingredients in a food processor until smooth. Mix all the soy dressing ingredients together.

Slice the tuna into 5 mm (¼ in) slices and arrange on 4 cold plates. The slices should slightly overlap and be to the side of the plates. Put a spoonful of the guacamole on each plate, again slightly to the side (off-setting food on plates makes it look more natural). Add a generous pool of the soy dressing and decorate the guacamole with a sprig of coriander.

grillade of tuna with olive oil mash

I cooked this when we were filming one of my television programmes, in Sourmiou, an idyllic beach just outside Marseilles in the Calanques. We arrived in Marseilles, typically, with no cooking equipment and nowhere to cook but we managed to borrow a *cabano*, a terracotta-tiled holiday cabin, just up from the beach, with a tiny kitchen to film in and a nice big terrace that had a glorious view over the limestone hills behind, dotted with wild thyme, mallow and great clumps of daisies. The fish in that case were sea bass and *daurade royale*, also known as gilt head bream, but tuna works well too, as do swordfish and shark. The dressing for the grillade is a difficult concept to grasp. I start with a simple, well-reduced, sharp tomato sauce and add lots of chopped aromatic herbs – what I loosely call Provençal herbs – in an olive oil and red wine vinegar dressing. The idea is that the finished dressing should look split, i.e. the tomato should appear to have separated from the dressing. It just looks much more fresh and appetizing than a smooth tomato sauce. Texture is very important visually as well as for the taste in my cooking.

SERVES 4

3 TABLESPOONS OLIVE OIL

LEAVES FROM 2 SPRIGS OF THYME

4 x 175 G (6 OZ) TUNA LOIN STEAKS

SEA SALT AND FRESHLY GROUND BLACK PEPPER

FOR THE TOMATO SAUCE:

1 MEDIUM ONION, FINELY CHOPPED

1 GARLIC CLOVE, FINELY CHOPPED

2 TABLESPOONS OLIVE OIL

400 G (14 OZ) CAN OF CHOPPED TOMATOES

50 ML (2 FL OZ) RED WINE VINEGAR

2 TEASPOONS CASTER SUGAR

FOR THE DRESSING:

120 ML (4 FL OZ) EXTRA VIRGIN OLIVE OIL

2 TABLESPOONS RED WINE VINEGAR

3 TABLESPOONS CHOPPED MIXED FRESH HERBS SUCH AS DILL, YOUNG
    BAY LEAF, THYME, ROSEMARY, OREGANO, SAVORY

1 TEASPOON SALT

FOR THE OLIVE OIL MASH:

900 G (2 LB) FLOURY POTATOES SUCH AS KING EDWARD, MARIS PIPER
    OR WILJA, PEELED AND CUT INTO CHUNKS

25 ML (1 FL OZ) DOUBLE CREAM

85 ML (3 FL OZ) OLIVE OIL

50 ML (2 FL OZ) *CHICKEN STOCK* (SEE P. 140)

2 GARLIC CLOVES, CRUSHED

½ TEASPOON SALT

METHOD

For the tomato sauce, fry the onion and garlic in the olive oil for 5 minutes, until softened. Add the chopped tomatoes and simmer for 15–20 minutes. Meanwhile, put the vinegar and sugar in a separate pan and boil down until reduced to about 1 teaspoon. Stir into the tomato sauce and season with salt and pepper.

Pass the sauce through a conical strainer into a clean pan. If necessary, simmer for a few minutes until the sauce is thick enough to coat the back of a spoon. (You only need half the sauce for this recipe, so set half aside and, when cool, keep in the fridge to use in another recipe.) Adjust the seasoning and keep warm.

For the dressing, put all the ingredients into a bowl, season with pepper and whisk together. Stir into the tomato sauce and keep warm.

For the olive oil mash, cook the potatoes in boiling salted water until tender, then drain. Add the cream, olive oil, chicken stock, garlic and salt and mash until smooth. Set aside and keep warm.

Place a lightly oiled cast-iron ribbed pan over a high heat. Mix the 3 tablespoons of olive oil with the thyme leaves. Brush the tuna with the thyme oil and season well with sea salt and pepper. When the pan is very hot, put the tuna on it and cook for about 4–5 minutes on each side, pressing down firmly with the back of a fish slice to help mark the fish with the lines from the griddle.

To serve, put the tuna on 4 warmed plates and spoon the olive oil mash to one side. Using a teaspoon, spoon little pools of the sauce to the other side of the fish.

seared tuna with rice noodles and coriander salad

I cooked this on my last trip to Australia after we'd been out on a yellowfin tuna boat off Ulludulla – can you think of a more Australian-sounding name than Ulludulla! This recipe sums up how I feel about Australian cooking at its best. The tuna is served very rare and the accompanying salad is designed to be served warm, not hot. I have suggested that you use three green chillies for this recipe because it needs to be quite punchy, but it will depend on how hot they are and how much you like chilli, so feel free to adjust this to your own taste.

SERVES 4

4 x 200 G (7 OZ) TUNA LOIN STEAKS

6 TABLESPOONS DARK SOY SAUCE

4 TABLESPOONS BALSAMIC VINEGAR

FOR THE RICE NOODLES AND CORIANDER SALAD:

1 TABLESPOON SESAME SEEDS

50 G (2 OZ) CORIANDER

6 SPRING ONIONS, TRIMMED

COARSELY GRATED ZEST AND JUICE OF 1 LIME

2 TABLESPOONS THAI FISH SAUCE (*NAM PLA*)

2 TEASPOONS ROASTED SESAME OIL

2 TABLESPOONS SUNFLOWER OIL

75 G (3 OZ) RICE VERMICELLI NOODLES

3 MEDIUM-HOT GREEN DUTCH CHILLIES, SEEDED AND FINELY CHOPPED

2 TABLESPOONS JAPANESE PICKLED GINGER, CUT INTO SHREDS

A SMALL BUNCH OF GARLIC CHIVES, CHOPPED (OPTIONAL)

A BUNCH OF WATERCRESS, LARGER STALKS REMOVED,
   BROKEN INTO SPRIGS

METHOD

For the salad, pre-heat the grill to high. Spread the sesame seeds on to a baking tray and toast, shaking the pan now and then, until golden. Pick the leaves off the coriander and discard the stalks – if the leaves are quite large, chop them very roughly. You will need about 6 tablespoons in all. Very thinly slice the spring onions on the diagonal. Mix together the lime juice, fish sauce, sesame oil, sunflower oil and 85 ml (3 fl oz) of water.

Bring a pan of water to the boil, drop in the noodles and take it off the heat. Leave to soak for 2 minutes, then drain well and tip the noodles back into the pan. Cover and keep warm. Heat a heavy-based frying pan until very hot. Brush with a little oil, add the tuna steaks and cook for 2 minutes on each side. Add the soy sauce and balsamic vinegar to the pan and boil vigorously, turning the steaks once, until they become coated in a rich brown glaze. Remove from the heat and keep warm while you finish the salad.

Add the sesame seeds, coriander, spring onions, lime zest, green chillies, pickled ginger, garlic chives, if using, and the watercress to the noodles. Add the dressing and toss everything together.

Pile some of the salad into the centre of 4 warmed plates, slice each tuna steak into 3 on the angle and rest on top of the salad. Serve the rest of the salad separately.

tonno con fagioli (tuna and cannellini beans)

This is often made with little more than the contents of two cans – tuna and beans. But if you use dried cannellini beans simmered with a bay leaf, shallot, garlic and thyme, and tuna slow-cooked with olive oil and herbs, you will produce something quite spectacularly better. This warm salad is finished with sliced red onion, parsley and extra virgin olive oil.

SERVES 4

225 G (8 OZ) DRIED CANNELLINI BEANS

1 BAY LEAF

1 SHALLOT, THINLY SLICED

2 SPRIGS OF THYME

1 GARLIC CLOVE, LEFT WHOLE,
   PLUS 1 SMALL GARLIC CLOVE, CRUSHED

85 ML (3 FL OZ) EXTRA VIRGIN OLIVE OIL, PLUS A LITTLE EXTRA TO SERVE

3 TABLESPOONS LEMON JUICE

1 SMALL RED ONION, THINLY SLICED

3 TABLESPOONS CHOPPED FLAT-LEAF PARSLEY,
   PLUS EXTRA TO GARNISH

SALT AND FRESHLY GROUND BLACK PEPPER

FOR THE TUNA CONFIT:

275 G (10 OZ) THICK TUNA LOIN STEAK

ABOUT 300 ML (10 FL OZ) INEXPENSIVE OLIVE OIL

1 ONION, THINLY SLICED

2 GARLIC CLOVES, SLICED

2 BAY LEAVES

¼ SMALL LEMON, SLICED

A LARGE SPRIG OF THYME

METHOD

Cover the beans with plenty of cold water and leave to soak overnight.

Make the tuna confit (if possible, do this the day before as well, so you can leave it for 24 hours to allow all the flavours to permeate the fish). Sprinkle a thin layer of salt in a shallow dish, lay the tuna on top and cover it with another layer of salt. Set aside for 10 minutes. Now brush most of the salt off the fish and rinse it under cold water. Dry on kitchen paper, then cut it, if necessary, into pieces that will fit neatly in a single layer in a small saucepan.

Heat 3 tablespoons of the oil in the pan, add the onion and garlic and fry gently for 5 minutes, until soft but not coloured. Add the bay leaves, lemon slices and thyme, put the tuna on top and then pour over the rest of the oil. If the oil does not cover the fish, add a little more. Place the pan over a low heat and slowly bring the temperature of the oil up to 100°C/212°F. Remove the pan from the heat and leave the tuna to cool.

Drain the beans, tip them into a large pan and add enough fresh water to cover them by about 2.5 cm (1 in). Bring to the boil and add the bay leaf, shallot, thyme and the whole clove of garlic. Simmer for about 45 minutes or until tender, topping them up with boiling water if necessary to make sure that they stay just covered.

Just as the beans are ready, return the tuna to a low heat and bring back up to 100°C/212°F. Drain the beans, discard the bay leaf, thyme and garlic and tip the beans into a bowl. Toss with the extra virgin olive oil, crushed garlic, lemon juice, some salt and plenty of pepper. Leave to cool slightly.

As soon as the tuna is back up to temperature, lift it out of the pan and allow the excess oil to drain away. Break the fish into chunky pieces and season them with ½ teaspoon of salt and pepper.

Toss the red onion and parsley into the beans and then carefully stir in the tuna so that you don't break up the flakes too much. Spoon into a large serving bowl, drizzle over a little extra olive oil and sprinkle with chopped parsley. Serve with plenty of crusty fresh bread.

3 trout, salmon & sardine dishes

marinated sea trout with lime and pink peppercorns ▪ **braised trout** with mint, parsley and caper sauce ▪ **pan-fried trout** with garlic and bacon ▪ **chargrilled lightly smoked sea trout** with chive dressing ▪ **chilli-glazed rainbow trout** with bok choy ▪ **braised fillet of sea trout** with basil, celeriac and chambéry ▪ **braised sea trout fillets** with white wine and basil ▪ **truite au bleu** with mousseline sauce ▪ **salmon rillettes** ▪ **gravlax** ▪ **salmon steaks** with muscadet, watercress and dill potatoes ▪ **salmon en croûte** with currants and ginger ▪ **escalopes of salmon** with a sorrel sauce ▪ **hot-smoked salmon sandwich** with crème fraîche and capers ▪ **whole salmon** baked in foil with tarragon ▪ **tians of lightly cured salmon** and avocado with a tomato and basil dressing ▪ **salmon fish cakes** with sorrel and watercress salad in a caper and lemon dressing ▪ **smoked salmon** with scrambled eggs ▪ **poached salmon** with mayonnaise, new potatoes and cucumber salad ▪ **grilled salmon** with curly kale and a noilly prat sauce ▪ **fried butterflied sardine fillets** with parmesan crumbs ▪ **escabèche of sardines** ▪ **sardine and potato curry puffs** ▪ **barbecued spiced sardines** with pilau rice

marinated sea trout with lime and pink peppercorns

This is a wonderful way of serving sea trout. Pink peppercorns are available nowadays in good delicatessens.

SERVES 4

1 x 225 G (8 OZ) PIECE OF UNSKINNED SEA TROUT FILLET

120 ML (4 FL OZ) SUNFLOWER OIL

10 G (¼ OZ) FRESH ROOT GINGER, VERY FINELY CHOPPED

1 TEASPOON PINK PEPPERCORNS IN BRINE, DRAINED AND RINSED

FINELY GRATED ZEST AND JUICE OF 1 LIME

½ TEASPOON SALT

METHOD

Put the sea trout fillet, skin-side down, on to a chopping board and thinly slice it at a 45° angle away from the skin with a very sharp, long-bladed knife as you would gravlax or smoked salmon.

Flatten the slices slightly and arrange them over the base of 4 dinner plates, overlapping them very slightly.

Mix together the rest of the ingredients. Five minutes before serving, drizzle the dressing over the fish and spread it out with the back of a teaspoon. Serve immediately.

braised trout with mint, parsley and caper sauce

It's a real pleasure to discover a really old recipe that has a modern feel about it. This particular recipe is just headed 'housekeeper's recipe' and is dated 1820. The extraordinary thing is that the sauce elements are like the very fashionable Italian sauce, salsa verde, and they have the same function – to partner a nice plump trout or freshwater pollan with some piquant flavours.

SERVES 4

4 RAINBOW TROUT, CLEANED (SEE P. 6)

50 ML (2 FL OZ) DRY WHITE WINE

50 ML (2 FL OZ) WATER

50 G (2 OZ) BUTTER

½ TABLESPOON MINT LEAVES

A SMALL BUNCH OF CHIVES

1½ TABLESPOONS FLAT-LEAF PARSLEY LEAVES

1½ TABLESPOONS CAPERS IN BRINE, DRAINED AND RINSED

3 ANCHOVY FILLETS IN OLIVE OIL, DRAINED

1 GARLIC CLOVE, ROUGHLY CHOPPED

½ TEASPOON DIJON MUSTARD

½ TEASPOON FRESH LEMON JUICE

1 TEASPOON PLAIN FLOUR

SALT AND FRESHLY GROUND BLACK PEPPER

METHOD

Pre-heat the oven to 200°C/400°F/Gas Mark 6.

Season the trout lightly inside and out and put them in a shallow baking dish. Pour over the wine and water and dot the fish here and there with half the butter. Cover with foil and bake for 25 minutes.

Meanwhile, pile the herbs, capers, anchovy fillets and garlic on to a board and chop together into a coarse paste. Scrape the mixture into a bowl and stir in the mustard and lemon juice.

Beat the remaining butter in a small bowl to soften it and then mix in the flour to make a smooth paste. Remove the trout from the oven and carefully pour off the cooking liquor into a small pan. Cover the trout again and keep them warm. Place the cooking liquor over a medium-high heat, bring it to a simmer and then whisk in the butter and flour paste. Leave it to simmer for 1 minute, stirring until smooth and thickened. Stir in the herb mixture and take the pan off the heat.

Put the trout on 4 warmed plates, spoon over the sauce and serve.

pan-fried trout with garlic and bacon

This is one of the straight-out-of-the-river-into-the-pan recipes which reminds me of a passage from Mark Twain's *Tom Sawyer:* 'They fried the fish with bacon and were astonished; for no fish had ever seemed so delicious before. They did not know that the quicker a fresh fish is on the fire after he is caught, the better.'

SERVES 4

4 x 225 G (8 OZ) TROUT, CLEANED (SEE P. 6)

FLOUR, FOR DUSTING

A SMALL KNOB OF BUTTER

25 ML (1 FL OZ) VEGETABLE OIL

6 RASHERS OF RINDLESS STREAKY BACON, CUT INTO THIN STRIPS

4 GARLIC CLOVES, CHOPPED

25 ML (1 FL OZ) *SHALLOT VINEGAR* (SEE P. 142)

1 TEASPOON FINELY CHOPPED PARSLEY

SALT AND FRESHLY GROUND BLACK PEPPER

METHOD

Season the fish inside and out with salt and pepper, then dust with flour, shaking off any excess. Melt the butter with the oil in a frying pan. Add the bacon and then the trout and fry for about 5 minutes on each side. Remove the trout and bacon from the pan and keep warm.

Turn down the heat, add the garlic and cook gently until soft. Pour the vinegar into the pan and bring to the boil. Add the chopped parsley, stir and pour over the fish. Serve immediately.

chargrilled lightly smoked sea trout with chive dressing

Smoked sea trout is cured in the same way as salmon: brined and then smoke-cured without heating. There is no need to cook the fillet through; it should be seared on the outside and just warm in the centre. Use a ribbed steak pan to get the sear marks. You can also use smoked salmon for this dish.

SERVES 4

350–450 G (12-16 OZ) PIECE OF SEA TROUT, SKINNED (SEE P. 6)

A SMALL BUNCH OF CHIVES

1 SMALL SHALLOT, FINELY CHOPPED

85 ML (3 FL OZ) EXTRA VIRGIN OLIVE OIL, PLUS EXTRA FOR BRUSHING

1 TABLESPOON WHITE WINE VINEGAR

½ TEASPOON SALT

HARDWOOD SAWDUST, FOR SMOKING

FOR THE LIGHT BRINE:

50 G (2 OZ) SALT

600 ML (1 PINT) WATER

METHOD

Make the brine by dissolving the salt in the water. Pour it into a shallow dish, add the sea trout fillet, cover and leave for 20 minutes.

To smoke the sea trout, put a 2.5 cm (1 in) layer of hardwood sawdust into the bottom of a wok or chef's pan. Rest 6 wooden chopsticks over the top of the sawdust, to act as a platform. Place the pan over a high heat until the sawdust starts to smoke, then reduce the heat to low.

Lift the sea trout fillet out of the brine and dry it on kitchen paper. Rest a sushi mat (or something else that is flat and permeable and will let the smoke through) on top of the chopsticks and lay the fish on top. Cover the wok or pan with a lid and smoke the fish for 3–4 minutes.

Remove the mat of fish from the pan and, with a palette knife, carefully lift the fish off the mat on to a board. Cut into 4 even-sized pieces.

For the chive dressing, set aside 4 of the chives for a garnish and finely chop the remainder. Mix them with the shallot, olive oil, vinegar and salt.

Heat a ridged cast-iron griddle until smoking-hot. Brush the pieces of sea trout with a little oil, place diagonally on to the griddle and cook for 30 seconds on each side until it is lightly marked by the ridges and the centre of the fish is just warm.

Spoon some of the dressing into the centre of 4 plates and put the pieces of sea trout on top. Garnish with the reserved chives and serve immediately.

chilli-glazed rainbow trout with bok choy

Because it's so easy to get hold of, we tend to underrate rainbow trout. It's a bit like parsley – if you tasted it for the first time I bet you'd be astounded by its subtle, delicate flavour. Trout is well flavoured and excellent value, but we use it so often that we take it for granted. When I thought this dish up I had in mind the flavours that the Chinese often put with carp, a subtle-flavoured fish, like trout. If you can't get bok choy, use pak choy. Steamed rice is all the accompaniment you'll need.

SERVES 2

2 x 350 G (12 OZ) RAINBOW TROUT, FILLETED (SEE P. 6-7) AND LEFT UNSKINNED

1 TABLESPOON SUNFLOWER OIL

3 TABLESPOONS DARK SOY SAUCE

2 TABLESPOONS BALSAMIC VINEGAR

1 SMALL GARLIC CLOVE, FINELY CHOPPED

1 CM (½ IN) FRESH ROOT GINGER, VERY FINELY CHOPPED

½ MEDIUM-HOT RED FINGER CHILLI, SEEDED AND FINELY CHOPPED

SALT AND FRESHLY GROUND BLACK PEPPER

A FEW SPRIGS OF CORIANDER, TO GARNISH

FOR THE BOK CHOY:

2 SMALL HEADS OF BOK CHOY OR OTHER CHINESE CABBAGE (TOTAL WEIGHT ABOUT 225 G/8 OZ), EACH HALVED LENGTHWAYS

¼ TEASPOON SESAME OIL, ROASTED OR PLAIN

1 CM (½ IN) FRESH ROOT GINGER, FINELY SHREDDED

½ TEASPOON CORNFLOUR

METHOD

For the bok choy, bring a pan of lightly salted water to the boil, tip in the bok choy halves and blanch for 3 minutes. Spoon 5 tablespoons of the cooking liquid into a small pan, then drain the bok choy, cover and keep warm.

Season the trout fillets lightly on both sides with salt and pepper. Heat the oil in a large frying pan over a high heat. Add the trout fillets and sear them for about 30 seconds on each side.

Take the frying pan off the heat and add the soy sauce, balsamic vinegar, garlic, ginger and chilli. Reduce the heat to medium, return the pan to the heat and cook on one side only for 3 minutes until the trout is just cooked through.

Meanwhile, add the sesame oil, shredded ginger and a pinch of salt to the reserved bok choy cooking liquid and mix the cornflour with 2 teaspoons of cold water. Bring the liquid to the boil, tip in the cornflour mixture and simmer, stirring, for 1 minute.

To serve, divide the bok choy between 2 warmed plates and rest 2 glazed trout fillets on top of each. Drizzle with the sauce, garnish with sprigs of coriander and serve immediately.

braised fillet of sea trout with
basil, celeriac and chambéry

Any dry white vermouth will do for this recipe if you can't get hold of Chambéry.

SERVES 4

100 G (4 OZ) UNSALTED BUTTER

175 G (6 OZ) CELERIAC, CUT INTO MATCHSTICKS

½ MEDIUM ONION, FINELY CHOPPED

120 ML (4 FL OZ) CHAMBÉRY OR OTHER DRY WHITE VERMOUTH

600 ML (1 PINT) *CHICKEN STOCK* (SEE P. 140)

4 x 200 G (7 OZ) UNSKINNED FILLETS OF SEA TROUT

6 FRESH BASIL LEAVES, THINLY SLICED

SALT AND FRESHLY GROUND WHITE PEPPER

METHOD

Melt the butter in a heavy pan, large enough for the fillets to be cooked side by side without overlapping too much. Add the celeriac and onion and soften for 2 minutes. Add the vermouth and half the chicken stock and simmer gently, covered, for about 10 minutes, then remove the lid.

Season the fillets with salt and pepper and place them in the pan on top of the vegetables. Pour in the rest of the chicken stock and sprinkle all but a final pinch of the basil over the top of the fish. Cover and braise very gently until the fish has just cooked.

Remove the sea trout from the pan and keep warm on a serving dish. Concentrate the flavour of the braised vegetables by turning the heat to high and boiling rapidly to reduce the volume by about half. Pour the contents of the pan around the fillets and garnish with the remaining basil.

Accompany with some fine beans and boiled potatoes.

braised sea trout fillets with white wine and basil

The idea for this dish came from a very early exploration of Michelin-starred restaurants in France. At the Moulin de Mougins near Lorient in Brittany I remember being particularly impressed by the use of basil in a butter sauce. It's easy to forget just how recently basil has become a common herb in the UK. Sometimes I wish it wasn't so easy to get everything from everywhere. I'll never be bowled over again by the fragrance of basil in a sauce – except perhaps the basil from my garden, which has so much more flavour than most of the shop-bought stuff.

SERVES 4

75 G (3 OZ) BUTTER

75 G (3 OZ) CARROTS, VERY THINLY SLICED

75 G (3 OZ) CELERY, VERY THINLY SLICED

75 G (3 OZ) LEEKS, VERY THINLY SLICED

85 ML (3 FL OZ) DRY WHITE WINE

600 ML (1 PINT) *CHICKEN STOCK* (SEE P. 140)

4 x 150 G (5 OZ) FILLETS OF SEA TROUT, SKINNED (SEE P. 6)

A HANDFUL BASIL LEAVES, VERY FINELY SHREDDED , PLUS SPRIGS

   OF BASIL, TO GARNISH

1 TEASPOON LEMON JUICE

SALT AND FRESHLY GROUND BLACK PEPPER

METHOD

Melt 50 g (2 oz) of the butter in a shallow pan large enough to hold the fish in 1 layer. Stir in the carrots, celery and leeks, cover and cook gently over a medium heat for about 3 minutes.

Add the wine and stock to the pan and simmer, uncovered, until almost all the liquid has evaporated but the vegetables are still moist.

Lay the sea trout fillets on top, season with some salt and pepper and sprinkle over half the shredded basil. Cover and simmer very gently for 8–10 minutes, or until the fish is just cooked through.

Put the fish on 4 warmed plates and keep warm. If there is a little too much liquid left in the pan, boil rapidly until the juices have reduced and the sauce is glistening. Stir in the rest of the butter, the lemon juice and the rest of the shredded basil and adjust the seasoning if necessary. Spoon the sauce over the fish and garnish with sprigs of basil.

truite au bleu with mousseline sauce

One summer we stayed at the Hotel Arcé in St Etienne de Baïgorry in the Pyrenees. Of course my boys took real delight in pronouncing its name wrongly. It was one of those family-run hotels where the family seem to do everything. Reception was a hatch between the restaurant and the kitchen and the chef (also the owner) would hand us our room key, deliver a message or take a booking. He also caught the trout for his *truite au bleu* in the stream in front of the restaurant. We would watch him wade through the shallow water and hook them out, one after the other. With this performance before dinner, we were sure not to be disappointed when we sat down to eat, and we weren't. The trout must be dropped into the simmering vinegary court bouillon very soon after they are killed so that their natural slime sets to give them a delicate slate-blue tinge.

SERVES 4

1 QUANTITY *BASIC COURT BOUILLON* (SEE P. 140)

750 G (1½ LB) TINY NEW POTATOES, SCRUBBED

4 x 275–350 G (10-12 OZ) TROUT, BOUGHT LIVE IF POSSIBLE OR
   KILLED WITHIN THE LAST HOUR, CLEANED (SEE P. 6)

1 TABLESPOON FINELY CHOPPED PARSLEY

SALT

FOR THE MOUSSELINE SAUCE:

½ QUANTITY *HOLLANDAISE SAUCE* OR *QUICK HOLLANDAISE SAUCE*
   (SEE P. 140–141)

25 ML (1 FL OZ) DOUBLE CREAM

METHOD

Bring the court bouillon to the boil in a shallow pan or casserole dish large enough to hold the trout in 1 layer, and simmer for 10 minutes.

Bring a pan of boiling salted water to the boil, allowing 1 teaspoon of salt for every pint of water. Add the potatoes and cook them for 15 minutes or until tender.

When the potatoes are about half-way through cooking, bring the court bouillon back to the boil, then turn off the heat and when the bubbles have subsided, slip in the trout. Leave them to poach for 7–8 minutes.

Meanwhile, for the mousseline sauce, first make the hollandaise sauce. Whip the cream until it just begins to form soft peaks. Gently fold it into the hollandaise sauce. Drain the potatoes and toss them with the chopped parsley. Carefully lift the trout out of the pan, drain well and serve with the potatoes and the mousseline sauce. For complete perfection, this should be accompanied by some freshly boiled young asparagus.

salmon rillettes

I first came across this dish in a restaurant near the rather unfortunately named town of Condom in south-west France. I suppose in Britain you might call it potted salmon, but rillettes seems more appropriate because the idea is to shred the salmon rather like duck or goose rillettes. Like its poultry counterpart it is designed to use valuable trimmings, such as the heads and tails, which would normally be thrown away but contain plenty of good-tasting fillet. It is flavoured with the sort of spices you would find in something like potted shrimps and served with a simple, fresh, green chutney made with capers, gherkins and herbs.

SERVES 4

100 G (4 OZ) BUTTER

1 TEASPOON SALT

2 SLICES OF LEMON

2 BAY LEAVES

10 BLACK PEPPERCORNS

350 G (12 OZ) UNSKINNED SALMON FILLET

¼ TEASPOON GROUND MACE

A GOOD PINCH OF GROUND ALLSPICE

FRESHLY GROUND WHITE PEPPER

WALNUT OR WHOLEMEAL BREAD

FOR THE CHUTNEY:

2 TEASPOONS ENGLISH MUSTARD POWDER

1 TABLESPOON CAPERS, DRAINED, RINSED AND FINELY CHOPPED

1 SMALL GHERKIN, CUT INTO FINE MATCHSTICKS (ABOUT 1 TABLESPOON)

1 TABLESPOON CHOPPED FRESH *FINES HERBES* (PARSLEY, CHERVIL, CHIVES AND TARRAGON)

2 TABLESPOONS EXTRA VIRGIN OLIVE OIL

1 TEASPOON WHITE WINE VINEGAR

½ TEASPOON SALT

METHOD

Leave the butter somewhere warm until it is really soft but not melted. Meanwhile, put 300 ml (10 fl oz) of water and the salt, lemon, bay leaves and peppercorns in a small pan, bring to the boil and simmer for 10 minutes. Add the salmon and simmer for 8–10 minutes. Leave to cool in the cooking water. Remove the skin and bones from the fish, place the flesh in a bowl and shred by pulling apart with 2 forks.

Add the butter to the salmon with the mace, allspice and 3 twists of pepper. Mix together gently with a fork, then cover and chill for 2 hours or until just firm. If it gets too hard, leave to soften at room temperature for about 30 minutes before serving.

For the green chutney, just mix together all the ingredients in a small bowl and season with pepper, then cover and chill. Serve the rillettes and chutney with lightly toasted walnut or wholemeal bread.

gravlax (dill-cured salmon)

The best cut of salmon for this dish, known in Scandinavia as gravlax, is the middle of the fish. Ask your fishmonger to cut the salmon in half lengthways and remove the bones. Clean it before beginning the marinating (see p. 6).

SERVES 6

2 x 750 G (1½ LB) UNSKINNED SALMON FILLETS

A LARGE BUNCH OF DILL, ROUGHLY CHOPPED

100 G (4 OZ) COARSE SEA SALT

75 G (3 OZ) WHITE SUGAR

2 TABLESPOONS CRUSHED WHITE PEPPERCORNS

FOR THE HORSERADISH AND MUSTARD SAUCE:

2 TEASPOONS FINELY GRATED HORSERADISH (FRESH OR FROM A JAR)

2 TEASPOONS FINELY GRATED ONION

1 TEASPOON DIJON MUSTARD

1 TEASPOON CASTER SUGAR

2 TABLESPOONS WHITE WINE VINEGAR

A GOOD PINCH OF SALT

175 ML (6 FL OZ) DOUBLE CREAM

METHOD

Put 1 of the salmon fillets, skin-side down, on to a large sheet of cling film. Mix the dill with the salt, sugar and crushed peppercorns and spread the mixture over the cut face of the salmon. Place the other fillet on top, skin-side up.

Tightly wrap the fish in 2 or 3 layers of cling film and lift it on to a large shallow tray. Rest a slightly smaller tray or chopping board on top of the fish and weight it down. Refrigerate for 2 days, turning the fish every 12 hours so that the briny mixture, which has developed inside the parcel, bastes the outside of the fish.

For the horseradish and mustard sauce, stir together all the ingredients except for the cream. Whip the cream into soft peaks, stir in the horseradish mixture, cover and chill.

To serve, remove the fish from the briny mixture and slice it at a 45° angle away from the skin with a very short, long-bladed knife, as you would smoked salmon. Arrange a few slices of the gravlax on each of 6 cold plates and serve with some of the sauce.

salmon steaks with muscadet, watercress and dill potatoes

In this recipe salmon steaks are fried briefly on both sides in clarified butter and then cooked in the oven until still slightly underdone. A sauce is made from the pan juices.

SERVES 4

750 G (1½ LB) LARGE NEW POTATOES, SCRUBBED

A SMALL BUNCH OF DILL

4 x 200 G (7 OZ) SALMON STEAKS

25 G (1 OZ) *CLARIFIED BUTTER* (SEE P. 142)

50 ML (2 FL OZ) MUSCADET OR ANOTHER DRY WHITE WINE

120 ML (4 FL OZ) *FISH STOCK* (SEE P. 140) OR *CHICKEN STOCK* (SEE P. 140)

50 G (2 OZ) UNSALTED BUTTER

1 TABLESPOON CHOPPED PARSLEY

75 G (3 OZ) WATERCRESS, LARGE STALKS REMOVED

2 TABLESPOONS EXTRA VIRGIN OLIVE OIL

1 TEASPOON WHITE WINE VINEGAR

SALT AND FRESHLY GROUND BLACK PEPPER

METHOD

Cut each potato lengthways into 4 or 6 pieces. Cook in boiling salted water with 2 sprigs of the dill for 10 minutes or until tender.

Meanwhile, pre-heat the oven to 200°C/400°F/Gas 6. Season the salmon steaks on both sides with salt and pepper. Heat the clarified butter in an ovenproof frying pan. Add the salmon and cook for 1–2 minutes on each side until lightly browned.

Remove the pan from the heat and leave to cool for 30 seconds. Then pour over the wine, transfer the pan to the oven and cook for 5 minutes.

Remove the salmon from the oven and lift the steaks on to a plate. Keep warm. For the sauce, pour the fish or chicken stock into the frying pan, bring to the boil and add the butter. Boil rapidly until the liquid has reduced by half. Add the parsley and adjust the seasoning if necessary.

To serve, arrange the salmon steaks, watercress and potatoes on 4 warmed plates. Mix together the olive oil, vinegar and ½ teaspoon of salt. Pour the dressing over the watercress, pour the sauce over the salmon and serve, garnished with the rest of the dill.

salmon en croûte with currants and ginger

George Perry-Smith brought this old English recipe up to date and made it one of his most famous restaurant dishes. George started the Hole in the Wall in Bath, then went on to open two restaurants in the West Country – the Carved Angel in Dartmouth and the Riverside at Helford in Cornwall. I mention people like him because I think they have been as influential in improving the standing of cooking and restaurants in Britain as cookery writers like Jane Grigson and Arabella Boxer. This dish is a hymn to a particularly British way with food.

SERVES 6

2 x 550 G (1¼ LB) PIECES OF SALMON FILLET, TAKEN FROM BEHIND
    THE GUT CAVITY OF A 3-4 KG (7-9 LB) FISH, SKINNED (SEE P. 6-7)
100 G (4 OZ) UNSALTED BUTTER, SOFTENED
4 PIECES OF STEM GINGER IN SYRUP, WELL DRAINED AND FINELY DICED
25 G (1 OZ) CURRANTS
½ TEASPOON GROUND MACE
750 G (1½ LB) CHILLED PUFF PASTRY
1 EGG, BEATEN
SALT AND FRESHLY GROUND BLACK PEPPER

METHOD

Season the salmon fillets well on both sides with salt. Mix the softened butter with the stem ginger, currants, mace, ½ teaspoon of salt and some pepper. Spread the inner face of 1 salmon fillet evenly with the butter mixture and then lay the second fillet on top.

Cut the pastry in half and, on a lightly floured surface, roll out 1 piece into a rectangle about 4 cm (1½ in) bigger than the salmon all the way around – approximately 18 x 33 cm (7 x 13 in). Roll out the second piece into a rectangle 5 cm (2 in) larger than the first one all the way round.

Lay the smaller rectangle of pastry on a well-floured baking tray and place the salmon in the centre. Brush a wide band of beaten egg around the salmon and lay the second piece of pastry on top, taking care not to stretch it. Press the pastry tightly around the outside of the salmon, trying to ensure that you have not trapped in too much air, and then press the edges together well.

Trim the edges of the pastry to leave a 2.5 cm (1 in) band all the way around. Brush this once more with egg. Mark the edge with a fork and decorate the top with a fish scale effect by pressing an upturned teaspoon gently into the pastry, working in rows down the length of the parcel. Chill for at least an hour.

Pre-heat the oven to 200°C/400°F/Gas 6 and put in a baking tray to heat up. Remove the salmon en croûte from the fridge and brush it with beaten egg.

Take the hot baking tray out of the oven and carefully transfer the salmon parcel on to it. Return it to the oven and bake for 35–40 minutes.

Remove the salmon from the oven and leave it to rest for 5 minutes. Transfer it to a warmed serving plate and take it to the table whole. Cut it across into slices and serve.

escalopes of salmon with a
sorrel sauce

The thin escalopes of salmon are cooked so quickly that they are almost raw inside. I find salmon and salmon trout, which you can use equally well in this recipe, disappointing when cooked right through, as they become dry.

SERVES 4

750 G (1½ LB) SALMON FILLET FROM A GOOD-SIZED SALMON,
  SKINNED (SEE P. 7)
2 TABLESPOONS SUNFLOWER OIL
SALT

FOR THE SORREL SAUCE:
600 ML (1 PINT) *FISH STOCK* (SEE P. 140)
175 ML (6 FL OZ) DOUBLE CREAM
50 ML (2 FL OZ) VERMOUTH (SUCH AS DRY MARTINI OR NOILLY PRAT)
25 G (1 OZ) SORREL LEAVES, WASHED AND DRIED
75 G (3 OZ) UNSALTED BUTTER
2 TEASPOONS LEMON JUICE

METHOD

Remove any bones from the fillet with tweezers, long-nosed pliers or by trapping them between the point of a small vegetable knife and your thumb.

With a sharp filleting knife or carving knife, cut the salmon into 12 slices about 5 mm (¼ in) thick. Cut on the slant down to the skin, angling your knife at about 45° so that you get wider slices. Brush a grilling tray with some of the sunflower oil and put in the 12 escalopes of salmon. Brush lightly with more of the oil and season with a little salt.

Pre-heat the grill to high and put 4 large plates in the oven to warm. Meanwhile make the sorrel sauce. Place the fish stock, half the cream and the vermouth in a pan and boil rapidly to reduce by three-quarters to about 175 ml (6 fl oz). Meanwhile, slice the sorrel leaves very thinly. When the fish stock has reduced, add the rest of the cream, the butter and the lemon juice. Reduce a little more then stir in all but a pinch of the sorrel.

Grill the escalopes for about 30 seconds to 1 minute. Spoon the sauce into the centre of 4 warmed plates. Carefully lift the escalopes from the grilling tray with a palette knife and overlap 3 escalopes on top of the sauce. Garnish with the remaining sorrel and serve.

hot-smoked salmon sandwich
with crème fraîche and capers

This recipe is served in our coffee shop in Padstow. You take some good bread such as sourdough, granary or ciabatta and toast it lightly, preferably on a cast-iron ribbed pan to give that slightly chargrilled flavour. Then you build up salad leaves on top of it with the salmon and a flavoured dressing and serve the sandwich with a knife and fork.

This has proved immensely successful for us and I think it's because it's the sort of light dish that everybody wants to eat these days. It is fantastic, particularly if you can get hold of hot-smoked salmon. This is salmon cured in the same way as smoked mackerel – in other words, it is actually smoked and cooked at the same time but then served cold. It is becoming more readily available but if you cannot get hold of it, use cold-smoked salmon instead.

SERVES 4

225 G (8 OZ) HOT-SMOKED SALMON

6 TABLESPOONS CRÈME FRAÎCHE

2 TABLESPOONS CAPERS, DRAINED, RINSED AND CHOPPED

1 TABLESPOON CHOPPED CHIVES

4 LARGE OR 8 SMALL SLICES OF SOURDOUGH OR OTHER CRUSTY WHITE BREAD

50 G (2 OZ) MIXED SALAD LEAVES SUCH AS ROCKET, CURLY ENDIVE, RADICCHIO, WATERCRESS AND OAKLEAF LETTUCE

SALT AND FRESHLY GROUND BLACK PEPPER

METHOD

Remove the skin and bones from the salmon and break the fish into large flakes. Mix the crème fraîche with the capers, chives and a little salt and pepper. Put a cast-iron ribbed pan over a high heat and, when hot, grill the slices of bread for 1 minute on each side. Cut each one diagonally into 3 and fan out slightly on 4 plates. Arrange the salmon, crème fraîche and salad leaves at random on top of the bread and serve immediately.

whole salmon baked in foil with tarragon

I wrote this recipe for the supermarket chain Tesco. I find them refreshingly open to criticism and willing to take on new suggestions. They have a very good supply of farmed salmon which they asked me to show off at its best, and I'm really pleased with this.

SERVES 4

50 G (2 OZ) BUTTER, MELTED

1 x 1.5 KG (3 LB) SALMON, CLEANED AND TRIMMED (SEE P. 6)

A SMALL BUNCH OF TARRAGON, ROUGHLY CHOPPED

120 ML (4 FL OZ) DRY WHITE WINE

JUICE OF ½ LEMON

SALT AND FRESHLY GROUND BLACK PEPPER

FOR THE *BEURRE BLANC*:

50 G (2 OZ) SHALLOTS, VERY FINELY CHOPPED

2 TABLESPOONS WHITE WINE VINEGAR

4 TABLESPOONS DRY WHITE WINE

6 TABLESPOONS *FISH STOCK* (SEE P. 140) OR WATER

2 TABLESPOONS DOUBLE CREAM

175 G (6 OZ) CHILLED BUTTER, CUT INTO SMALL PIECES

FRESHLY GROUND WHITE PEPPER

METHOD

Pre-heat the oven to 220°C/425°F/Gas 7. Brush the centre of a large sheet of foil with some of the melted butter. Place the salmon in the centre and bring the edges of the foil slightly up around the fish. Put the open parcel on to a large baking tray.

Mix the tarragon with the rest of the melted butter, plus the wine, lemon juice, salt and pepper. Spoon the mixture into the cavity of the fish and over the top. Bring the sides of the foil up over the fish and pinch together, folding over the edges a few times to make a loose airtight parcel. Bake for 30 minutes.

Meanwhile, make the *beurre blanc*. Put the shallots, vinegar, wine and stock or water into a small pan and simmer until nearly all the liquid has evaporated. Add the cream and boil until reduced a little more. Lower the heat and gradually whisk in the butter, a few pieces at a time, until the sauce has amalgamated. Season to taste with salt and white pepper.

Remove the fish from the oven and open up the parcel. If you wish, remove the skin as follows: cut through the skin just behind the head and above the tail and lift it off. Carefully turn the fish over and repeat on the other side.

Lift the salmon on to a warmed serving dish and serve with the *beurre blanc* and some boiled new potatoes.

tians of lightly cured salmon
and avocado with a tomato and basil dressing

Smoked and raw salmon are shaped into small discs between which are sandwiched some slices of avocado. The salmon is flavoured with lemon juice, garlic and shallots and accompanied by a sauce of lemon juice, tomato, basil and virgin olive oil. Since the salmon is not cooked, it is essential that it is just mixed together, moulded and then served so that it all tastes of itself. Serve as a first course or maybe as something exceptional to eat outdoors with that special glass of white wine from the Loire.

SERVES 4

400 G (14 OZ) SALMON FILLET, SKINNED (SEE P. 7)

100 G (4 OZ) SMOKED SALMON

1 LARGE GARLIC CLOVE, VERY FINELY CHOPPED

3 SHALLOTS, VERY FINELY CHOPPED

1½ TABLESPOONS LEMON JUICE

12 TURNS OF THE BLACK PEPPER MILL

A PINCH OF CAYENNE PEPPER

A FEW DROPS OF WORCESTERSHIRE SAUCE

2 SMALL AVOCADOS

SALT

MIXED BABY SALAD LEAVES, TO GARNISH

FOR THE DRESSING:

50 ML (2 FL OZ) EXTRA VIRGIN OLIVE OIL

1 TABLESPOON LEMON JUICE

2 TOMATOES, SKINNED, SEEDED AND FINELY DICED

½ TEASPOON COARSE SEA SALT

8 BASIL LEAVES, VERY FINELY SHREDDED

A FEW TURNS OF THE BLACK PEPPER MILL

METHOD

Thinly slice the salmon fillet and smoked salmon, then cut them into strips about 5 mm (¼ in) wide. Put them in a bowl with the garlic, shallots, 1 tablespoon of the lemon juice, ½ teaspoon of salt, black pepper, cayenne pepper and Worcestershire sauce and mix together well. Halve the avocados and remove the stone and peel. Cut each half into thin slices, then mix with the remaining lemon juice and a pinch of salt. Place a 9 cm (3½ in) poaching ring or plain pastry cutter in the centre of each of 4 large plates. Divide half the salmon mixture between the rings and lightly level the top; don't press the mixture down – you want it to be loosely packed. Cover each one with avocado slices and then with the remaining salmon mixture, lightly levelling the top once more. Carefully remove the rings.

For the dressing, lightly stir the ingredients together in a bowl. Arrange 4 small piles of the salad leaves around each tian. Using a teaspoon, spoon little pools of the dressing in between the leaves and then serve.

salmon fish cakes with sorrel and watercress salad in a caper and lemon dressing

These fish cakes have plenty of fresh tarragon in them, which goes very well with salmon I always think, and they're served with a simple salad and quite a sharp dressing to cut the richness of the deep-frying. If you can't get sorrel leaves, don't worry, just use some other small salad leaves, but sorrel does add a slightly tart accent which is most pleasing with the fish cakes.

SERVES 4

900 G (2 LB) POTATOES, PEELED AND CUT INTO CHUNKS

750 G (1½ LB) COOKED SALMON

25 G (1 OZ) BUTTER, MELTED

1 TABLESPOON CHOPPED TARRAGON

15 G (½ OZ) CHOPPED PARSLEY

1 TEASPOON SALT

SUNFLOWER OIL, FOR DEEP-FRYING

50 G (2 OZ) PLAIN FLOUR, SEASONED WITH SALT AND PEPPER

2 EGGS, BEATEN

150 G (5 OZ) FRESH WHITE BREADCRUMBS

15 G (½ OZ) SORREL LEAVES, TORN INTO SMALL PIECES

15 G (½ OZ) WATERCRESS, DIVIDED INTO SPRIGS

FRESHLY GROUND BLACK PEPPER

FOR THE CAPER AND LEMON DRESSING:

JUICE OF 1 SMALL LEMON

85 ML (3 FL OZ) OLIVE OIL

2 TABLESPOONS CAPERS, DRAINED, RINSED AND FINELY CHOPPED

1 SMALL GARLIC CLOVE, CRUSHED

1 TABLESPOON CHOPPED CHIVES

1 TABLESPOON CHOPPED DILL OR FENNEL HERB

METHOD

Cook the potatoes in boiling salted water until tender. Drain well, tip back into the pan and mash until smooth. Leave to cool slightly.

Break the salmon into small flakes, removing any bones and skin. Put into a bowl with the mashed potatoes, melted butter, herbs, salt and some black pepper. Mix together well. Shape the mixture into 8 rounds about 2.5 cm (1 in) thick, cover with cling film and chill for 20 minutes.

Meanwhile, whisk all the ingredients for the dressing together and season to taste.

Pour the oil into a pan until it is no more than half full and heat to 180°C/350°F or until a small piece of white bread dropped into the oil browns and rises to the surface in 1 minute. Dip the fish cakes into the seasoned flour, then the beaten eggs and finally the breadcrumbs, pressing them on well to give an even coating. Deep-fry a batch of fish cakes for about 4 minutes, until crisp and golden. Lift out and drain briefly on kitchen paper. Keep warm in a low oven while you cook the rest.

Toss the sorrel and watercress with 1 tablespoon of the dressing. Put the fish cakes on 4 warmed plates, pile the dressed salad leaves to one side and spoon a little more dressing over the remainder of the plate.

smoked salmon with scrambled eggs

Smoked salmon with scrambled eggs is for the sort of breakfast at which you will also be drinking champagne with one of those euphoric hangovers after an evening which was quite special. On reflection, you'd better get somebody else to make it!

SERVES 4

4 THIN SLICES OF BROWN BREAD

100 G (4 OZ) UNSALTED BUTTER

12 EGGS

½ TEASPOON SALT

FRESHLY GROUND BLACK PEPPER

25 ML (1 FL OZ) DOUBLE CREAM

100 G (4 OZ) THINLY SLICED SMOKED SALMON

METHOD

Toast the 4 slices of brown bread, spread thinly with some of the butter, then cut off the crusts. Now cut each piece of buttered toast into 6 'triangles' but cutting off each corner of the square midway between one corner and the next. Cut the small square of toast that remains in half. (Eating the scrambled egg is much easier when it's resting on neatly cut small pieces of toast.)

Break the eggs into a bowl and whisk together with the salt and pepper. Melt the remaining butter in a pan and add the eggs. Stir with a wooden spoon scraping the cooked egg away from the bottom of the pan all the time until the degree of firmness that you like is achieved; I prefer the eggs to be a little runny.

Remove the pan from the heat and stir in the double cream. Fold the smoked salmon into the scrambled eggs and serve on the buttered toast.

poached salmon with mayonnaise, new potatoes and cucumber salad

Well-produced farmed salmon is perfectly acceptable for this dish but even more delightful is wild salmon. I'd far sooner you cooked with farmed fish, than not at all. If you prefer, you can use sea trout, a brown trout which has exchanged its habitat of rivers for the open sea. Its flesh develops a pink colour from a diet of crustaceans but is slightly less pronounced than salmon. Salmon and sea trout taste far better if eaten slightly underdone than overcooked, and if using in this recipe should be served warm not hot.

SERVES 4

1 QUANTITY *BASIC COURT BOUILLON* (SEE P. 140)

1 x 1.5–1.75 KG (3–4 LB) SALMON, CLEANED (SEE P. 6)

750 G (1½ LB) NEW POTATOES, SCRAPED

3 SPRIGS OF MINT

1 CUCUMBER

1 TABLESPOON WHITE WINE VINEGAR

1 QUANTITY *MAYONNAISE* (SEE P. 141), MADE WITH OLIVE OIL

SALT

METHOD

Bring the court bouillon to the boil in a fish kettle or oval casserole dish. Reduce to a simmer. Place the salmon on a trivet or upturned plate and carefully lower it into the court bouillon, bring back to a gentle simmer and poach gently for 16–18 minutes.

Meanwhile, boil the potatoes in salted water with 1 of the mint sprigs until tender, then drain and keep warm.

Peel the cucumber and slice it as thinly as possible, preferably on a mandolin. Chop the leaves from the remaining mint sprigs and mix with the cucumber, the vinegar and a pinch of salt.

Lift the salmon, still sitting on the trivet or plate, out of the fish kettle or casserole dish and allow any excess water to drain away. Carefully lift it off the trivet or plate with 2 fish slices and put it on a serving plate.

Remove the skin by making a shallow cut through the skin along the backbone and around the back of the head and carefully peeling it back. Carefully turn the fish over and repeat on the other side.

To serve, run a knife down the length of the fish between the 2 fillets and gently ease them apart and away from the bones. Lift portion-sized pieces of the salmon on to each of 4 warmed plates, then turn the fish over and repeat. Serve with the new potatoes, mayonnaise and cucumber salad.

grilled salmon with curly kale and a noilly prat sauce

Salmon was perceived until the 1970s as being a bit of a luxury, but thanks to fish farming, it is now cheaper and more widely available. Indeed, its popularity has given people a real taste for fish. Salmon has loads of flavour and an attractive colour – and it suits cooking in almost any way.

SERVES 4

4 x 175-200 G (6-8 OZ) PIECES OF 2.5 CM (1 IN) THICK SALMON FILLET,
    SKINNED (SEE P. 7)
50 G (2 OZ) BUTTER, MELTED
150 G (5 OZ) CURLY KALE, SHREDDED
SALT AND FRESHLY GROUND BLACK PEPPER

FOR THE SAUCE:
600 ML (1 PINT) *FISH STOCK* (SEE P. 140)
4 TABLESPOONS DOUBLE CREAM
4 TABLESPOONS NOILLY PRAT (DRY WHITE VERMOUTH)
75 G (3 OZ) CHILLED UNSALTED BUTTER, CUT INTO SMALL PIECES
1 TEASPOON THYME

METHOD

Pre-heat the grill to high. For the sauce, pour the stock, cream and Noilly Prat into a medium-sized pan and boil rapidly until reduced by three-quarters. Turn off the heat and keep warm.

Brush the salmon on all sides with half the melted butter and season with salt and pepper. Place on a lightly buttered baking tray and grill for 8 minutes until just cooked through.

While the salmon is cooking, bring a large pan of salted water to the boil, add the kale and cook for 3–4 minutes. Remove, drain well and return to the pan, then add the remaining melted butter and toss. Cover the pan to keep warm.

Bring the sauce to a simmer, then whisk in the chilled butter 1 piece at a time. Stir in the thyme and season to taste.

To serve, divide the kale between 4 warmed plates and top each with a piece of salmon. Spoon some of the sauce over the fish and the rest around the kale. Serve with some steamed new potatoes and pass round any remaining sauce in a small jug.

fried butterflied sardine fillets
with parmesan crumbs

The heads are removed from whole sardines and most of the backbone is taken out, leaving an inch or so at the tail end, which gives the deep-fried fish a very pretty shape. The process of removing the bones is easier if the sardines are fresh but this is not a recipe where frozen fish need be ruled out. The delight is the remarkably pleasant, crisp Parmesan and parsley crust sandwiching a moist but thin sheet of sardine fillet – served with nothing more than lemon wedges.

SERVES 4

12 SARDINES, SCALED

40 G (1½ OZ) FINELY GRATED PARMESAN CHEESE

1½ TABLESPOONS CHOPPED PARSLEY

50 G (2 OZ) FRESH WHITE BREADCRUMBS

50 G (2 OZ) PLAIN FLOUR

2 EGGS, BEATEN

SUNFLOWER OIL, FOR DEEP-FRYING

SALT AND FRESHLY GROUND BLACK PEPPER

SPRIGS OF FLAT-LEAF PARSLEY, TO GARNISH (OPTIONAL)

LEMON WEDGES

METHOD

First butterfly the sardines (see below).

Pre-heat the oven to 150°C/300°F/Gas 2. Line a baking tray with plenty of kitchen paper.

Mix together the Parmesan, chopped parsley, breadcrumbs and some salt and pepper. Dip the butterflied sardines into the flour, then into the beaten egg and finally into the breadcrumb mixture, pressing it on well to give an even coating.

Pour the oil into a large pan and heat to 180°C/350°F or until a small piece of white bread dropped into the oil browns and rises to the surface in about 1 minute. Deep-fry 1 or 2 sardines for 1 minute, flipping them over half-way through so that they brown on both sides. Lift out with a slotted spoon on to the paper-lined tray and keep hot in the oven while you cook the rest. Garnish with sprigs of parsley, if you like, and serve with lemon wedges.

butterflying sardines

1 Trim the fins off the sardines with kitchen scissors. Cut off the heads and then cut along the belly from the gut cavity right down to the tail and pull out the guts with your fingers.

2 Open out each fish and place, belly-side down, on a chopping board. Gently but firmly press along the backbone with your thumb or the palm of your hand, so that you gradually flatten out the fish.

3 Turn the fish over and carefully pull out the backbone, snipping it off at the tail end with scissors. Remove any small bones that are left behind with a pair of tweezers or pliers.

escabèche of sardines

Although the word *escabèche* is of Spanish origin, this is a classic Provençal dish, reflecting the fact that fish is cooked in this way all around the Mediterranean. First the fish is fried in olive oil, then a hot marinade of red wine vinegar, chilli, garlic, herbs and, in Provence, orange peel, is poured over it. I have added some roughly chopped flat-leaf parsley to produce a simple and delightful dish. I made this in Marseilles under the critical eye of Madame Forte, whose *cabano*, a charming old-fashioned beach chalet, I had borrowed while an episode of my television series, *Fruits of the Sea*, was being filmed. Monsieur Forte assured me that his wife had made *escabèche* all her life and knew everything there was to know about it. She pronounced mine too vinegary and without enough olive oil. I have since made these essential adjustments and hope that she'll try it again and approve.

SERVES 4

12 SARDINES, CLEANED (SEE P. 6)

50 G (2 OZ) PLAIN FLOUR, SEASONED WITH SALT AND PEPPER

150 ML (5 FL OZ) OLIVE OIL

85 ML (3 FL OZ) RED WINE VINEGAR

1 MEDIUM ONION, THINLY SLICED

5 CM (2 IN) STRIP OF PARED ORANGE ZEST

A SPRIG OF THYME

A SPRIG OF ROSEMARY

1 BAY LEAF

4 GARLIC CLOVES, CRUSHED

2 DRIED RED CHILLIES

A SMALL BUNCH OF FLAT-LEAF PARSLEY, ROUGHLY CHOPPED

SALT

METHOD

Remove the heads from the sardines, then dust them in the seasoned flour. Fry them in half the olive oil for 1 minute on each side, then transfer to a shallow dish.

Add the vinegar, onion, orange zest, thyme, rosemary, bay leaf, garlic, chillies and 1 teaspoon of salt to the pan, bring to the boil and simmer for about 15 minutes.

Add the rest of the olive oil and the parsley, pour the hot marinade over the sardines and leave until cold.

sardine and potato curry puffs

Oily fish such as sardines and herrings are only great grilled whole if they are extremely fresh – 'stiff fresh', as they say in the fishmongering trade. Some of the previously frozen sardines sold at supermarket counters and labelled 'suitable for barbecuing' are, in my opinion, only suitable for adding to the barbecue as fuel. But the same sardines, or even mackerel, trout and herrings, that aren't tip-top for grilling are ideal for a hot, robustly flavoured dish like this. The point is that the oil in the fish will develop more flavour as the fish ages.

MAKES 12

100 G (4 OZ) POTATOES, PEELED AND CUT INTO 1 CM (½ IN) CUBES

1 TABLESPOON GROUNDNUT OR SUNFLOWER OIL, PLUS EXTRA FOR DEEP-FRYING

2 GARLIC CLOVES, CRUSHED

1 CM (½ IN) FRESH ROOT GINGER, FINELY GRATED

½ ONION, THINLY SLICED

1 TABLESPOON *GOAN MASALA PASTE* (SEE P. 142) OR GOOD-QUALITY GARAM MASALA PASTE

225 G (8 OZ) SARDINES, CLEANED AND FILLETED (SEE P. 6–7) AND CUT ACROSS INTO STRIPS 2.5 CM (1 IN) WIDE

1 MEDIUM-HOT RED DUTCH CHILLI, SEEDED AND FINELY CHOPPED

1 TABLESPOON LEMON JUICE

¼ TEASPOON SALT

2–3 SPRING ONIONS, SLICED

2 TABLESPOONS CHOPPED CORIANDER

450 G (1 LB) CHILLED PUFF PASTRY

LEMON WEDGES AND SPRIGS OF CORIANDER, TO GARNISH

METHOD

Boil the potato cubes in salted water until just tender, then drain. Heat 1 tablespoon of the oil in a large frying pan and fry the garlic, ginger and onion for 1 minute. Add the masala paste and fry for 1 minute, then add the pieces of sardine and fry for another minute. Finally add the potato, chilli, lemon juice and salt and cook for 1 minute. Take the pan off the heat, stir in the spring onions and coriander and leave to cool.

Roll out the pastry on a lightly floured surface and cut out twelve 10 cm (4 in) circles. Spoon a heaped teaspoon of the filling mixture on to each circle. Brush half of the pastry edge with a little water, then fold it over the filling and press together well to seal the edge. Mark along the edge with a fork to make an even tighter seal.

Heat some oil for deep-frying to 190°C/375°F or until a small piece of white bread dropped into the oil browns and rises in 1 minute. Deep-fry 3 or 4 puffs for 7–8 minutes, turning them over every now and then, until they are golden brown. Drain on kitchen paper. Keep warm in a low oven while you cook the rest. Pile them on a plate and serve warm, garnished with some lemon wedges and sprigs of coriander.

barbecued spiced sardines with pilau rice

Much as I love simply grilled sardines and pilchards straight off the barbecue, I also enjoy them cooked in the same way but stuffed with a little intensely aromatic Goan masala paste. And the pilau rice cooked by my friend Rui in Goa is to die for! However, there's such a difference between fresh and frozen sardines that I must say here that this dish should only be made with fresh ones. A fresh sardine, still firm and, as the Cornish say, 'sweet as a nut', is a delight. Barbecued frozen sardines are such a disappointment, you're left thinking how horrible oily fish are, when in fact it isn't true.

SERVES 4

12 SARDINES, CLEANED AND FILLETED (SEE P. 6-7)

1 QUANTITY *GOAN MASALA PASTE* (SEE P. 142)

1 QUANTITY *KACHUMBER SALAD* (SEE P. 140), TO SERVE

FOR THE PILAU RICE:

SUNFLOWER OIL, FOR FRYING

6 LARGE SHALLOTS, THINLY SLICED

3 CLOVES

3 GREEN CARDAMOM PODS

5 CM (2 IN) PIECE OF CINNAMON STICK

1 BAY LEAF

350 G (12 OZ) BASMATI RICE

SALT

METHOD

Pre-heat the barbecue. Cut the heads off the sardines and then fillet them (see p. 6), leaving them attached at the tail end. Spread the cut face of 1 fillet with a teaspoon of the masala paste. Push the fish back into shape and tie in place, at what was the head end, with some string. Repeat with the remaining sardines.

For the pilau rice, heat a good deep layer of oil in a large frying pan. Add the shallots and fry, stirring now and then, until crisp and golden. Lift out with a slotted spoon on to plenty of kitchen paper and leave to drain.

Heat 2 tablespoons of oil in a large pan, add the cloves, green cardomom pods, cinnamon stick and bay leaf and cook for a few seconds until they start to smell aromatic. Stir in the rice, ½ teaspoon of salt and 600 ml (1 pint) of water, bring to the boil, then cover and cook over a low heat for 10 minutes.

Remove the rice from the heat and leave for another 5 minutes. Meanwhile, place the sardines on the barbecue and cook them for 1–2 minutes on each side, until crisp and lightly golden. Toss the fried shallots with a little salt and then stir them into the cooked rice. Serve with the sardines and kachumber salad.

4 prawn & scallop dishes

salad of prawns, rocket and parma ham ■ prawn cocktail with malt whisky ■ prawns fried with garlic butter ■ nasi goreng ■ po' boys ■ tiger prawn and avocado salad ■ deep-fried prawn wontons with chilli jam ■ stir-fried prawns ■ north atlantic prawn pilaf ■ prawn caldine ■ tandoori prawns ■ stir-fried salt and pepper prawns ■ pad thai noodles with prawns ■ grilled dublin bay prawns with a pernod and olive oil dressing ■ prawn-stuffed papads ■ gremolata prawns ■ prawn jambalaya ■ paper-wrapped prawns in honey and ginger ■ fritto misto di mare ■ chargrilled tiger prawns with lemongrass, chilli and coriander ■ sautéed scallops with basil, saffron and pasta ■ steamed scallops in the shell with ginger, soy, sesame oil and spring onions ■ seared scallops with Ibérico ham ■ scallops with noisette butter ■ sautéed scallops with lentils and chardonnay ■ scallops with duck livers and spaghettini ■ seared scallop salad with parma ham and croûtons ■ sautéed scallops with caramelized chicory

salad of prawns, rocket and parma ham

The supreme strength of Italian cuisine is that the unique flavours of the ingredients are presented in such a way that they enhance but do not smother each other. All the flavours in this salad are interesting on their own, but drawn together with some good olive oil they produce an effect greater than the sum of their parts.

SERVES 4

6 VERY THIN SLICES OF PARMA HAM

50 G (2 OZ) ROCKET LEAVES

100 G (4 OZ) LARGE COOKED PEELED PRAWNS

4 TABLESPOONS EXTRA VIRGIN OLIVE OIL

FRESHLY GROUND BLACK PEPPER

METHOD

Tear the Parma ham into pieces about 5 cm (2 in) across. Divide the rocket leaves between 4 cold plates and arrange the Parma ham among the leaves. Scatter over the prawns then drizzle 1 tablespoon of the olive oil over each salad. Finally, grind over some black pepper and serve with a bottle of chilled white Pinot Grigio.

prawn cocktail with malt whisky

There is no substitute for tomato ketchup for a prawn cocktail, no fresh tomato sauce ever tastes so good. However, the other ingredients can make all the difference. The difference here is malt whisky, which gives the prawn cocktail a subtle aftertaste of open log fires: just the thing for Christmas. In this recipe I have included a small amount of natural yoghurt, which gives the sauce a subtle extra tartness. If, as I do, you love prawn cocktails, make them big, particularly for a special occasion. Go to a glassware shop and buy some really voluminous glasses. The glasses we use are large and no attempt is made to fill them although the portions in this recipe are generous.

SERVES 4

225 G (8 OZ) LARGE FROZEN PEELED NORTH ATLANTIC PRAWNS

FOR THE MARIE ROSE SAUCE:

5 TABLESPOONS TOMATO KETCHUP

4 TABLESPOONS GREEK-STYLE NATURAL YOGHURT

2 TABLESPOONS MALT WHISKY

1 QUANTITY *MAYONNAISE* (SEE P. 141) MADE WITH SUNFLOWER OIL

SALT AND FRESHLY GROUND WHITE PEPPER

FOR THE SALAD:

90 G (3½ OZ) MIXED SALAD LEAVES INCLUDING, IF POSSIBLE,
  SOME RADICCHIO

4 BASIL LEAVES, THINLY SLICED

METHOD

Defrost the prawns overnight in the refrigerator and chill 4 large glasses.

Stir the tomato ketchup, yoghurt, malt whisky and some salt and pepper into the mayonnaise.

Tear the salad leaves into pieces no more than 5 cm (2 in) across and divide between the chilled glasses. Place the prawns gently on top so that they cover the salad but leave a gap around the circumference of the glass.

Pour the sauce over the prawns without totally covering all of either them or the salad. The dish looks much more appetizing if you can see a few pink pieces of uncovered prawn and some uncoated leaves. Finally put a little pile of sliced basil leaves in the centre of each glass.

prawns fried with garlic butter

There is really very little to this recipe except a first-rate set of ingredients but it's just one of those dishes that is totally irresistible and can be knocked up in, let us say, five minutes flat.

SERVES 4

2 LARGE GARLIC CLOVES, PEELED

100 G (4 OZ) UNSALTED BUTTER, SOFTENED

1 TEASPOON LEMON JUICE

1 TEASPOON BRANDY

24 LARGE COOKED UNSHELLED PRAWNS

15 G (½ OZ) CHOPPED PARSLEY

SALT AND FRESHLY GROUND BLACK PEPPER

METHOD

For the garlic butter, roughly chop the garlic cloves, then add a good pinch of salt and crush to a paste with the back of a knife. Mix with the butter, lemon juice and brandy.

Melt 25 g (1 oz) of the garlic butter in a large frying pan. Add the prawns and gently fry for 2 minutes or until they are heated through. Season with salt and pepper. Stir the chopped parsley into the remaining garlic butter, add to the pan and, when it has melted and is hot and foaming, spoon the prawns into 4 warmed gratin dishes. Serve immediately, with lots of freshly baked French bread to mop up the garlic butter.

nasi goreng

The secret of a good nasi goreng is rice that has been cooked well so that the grains are separate, and which has been left to cool but not refrigerated. Leftover rice that has been stored in the fridge overnight does not taste as good. Like so many rice or noodle street dishes from South-east Asia, nasi goreng is a bit of a 'put whatever you like into it' sort of dish. However, it should always include a good curry paste, some thinly sliced omelette and plenty of crisp fried onion flakes. I always put prawns in my nasi goreng, but I also love some broken-up well-flavoured fish like mackerel as an alternative. This dish is a perfect accompaniment to the *Malaysian Fried Lemon Sole* on page 46.

SERVES 4

2 EGGS

2 TEASPOONS SESAME OIL

½ TEASPOON SALT

2 TABLESPOONS SUNFLOWER OIL

2 GARLIC CLOVES, VERY FINELY CHOPPED

2.5 CM (1 IN) FRESH ROOT GINGER, VERY FINELY CHOPPED

6 SPRING ONIONS, WHITE AND GREEN SEPARATED, THINLY SLICED

100 G (4 OZ) COOKED PEELED PRAWNS

1 TABLESPOON CHOPPED CORIANDER

FOR THE BAKED RICE:

175 G (6 OZ) LONG-GRAIN RICE SUCH AS THAI JASMINE OR BASMATI

A SMALL KNOB OF BUTTER

½ TEASPOON SALT

350 ML (12 FL OZ) BOILING WATER

METHOD

Pre-heat the oven to 200°C/400 °F/Gas 6.

First make the baked rice. Wash the rice in cold water until the water runs clear. Melt the butter in a flameproof casserole dish, add the rice, salt and water and bring to the boil. Cover with a tight-fitting lid or foil, and bake in the oven for 15 minutes. Set aside.

Beat the eggs with the sesame oil and salt. Heat the oil in a wok or a large frying pan, add the garlic, ginger and the white part of the spring onions and stir-fry for about 3 minutes, until golden. Add the beaten eggs and stir-fry for 1 minute. Add the cooked rice and stir until it is thoroughly heated through, then add the prawns and heat through. Finally, sprinkle over the green spring onion tops and the coriander, then serve.

po' boys

I think we tend to dismiss American fast food as (a) bad for you, (b) made out of junk and (c) unsubtle. But because there's so much rubbish around, do we sometimes miss the real gems? Fast food like these po' boys, for example, in no way subtle and made out of good wholesome ingredients, goes straight to the heart of what you sometimes want, just like a great rock 'n' roll song. When the Americans get fast food right, like this dish, nobody does it better! As the name might suggest, po' boys originated as food for the poor, or at least that's what most of the explanations of the name suggest. The most plausible to me is that it originated in New Orleans in the nineteenth century as an oyster sandwich which was given as charity to the poor. Though oysters were the original filling, po' boys are made with both prawns and clams as well.

MAKES 6

2 BAGUETTES

SUNFLOWER OIL FOR DEEP-FRYING

350 G (12 OZ) RAW PEELED PRAWNS

175 G (6 OZ) *MAYONNAISE* (SEE P. 141) MADE WITH SUNFLOWER OIL,
    PLUS EXTRA TO SERVE

2½ TABLESPOONS MILK

25 G (1 OZ) PLAIN FLOUR

175 G (6 OZ) FRESH WHITE BREADCRUMBS

1 SMALL CRISP GREEN LETTUCE

SALT AND CAYENNE PEPPER

METHOD

Cut each baguette into 3 and then cut each piece in half lengthways. Pull out a little of the soft white crumb to make a very shallow dip in each half. Lay the bread on a baking tray, cut-side up, and toast very lightly under the grill. Remove and set aside.

Heat some oil for deep-frying to 190°C/375°F or until a small piece of white bread dropped into the oil browns and rises in 1 minute. Season the prawns well with salt and cayenne pepper. Whisk the mayonnaise and milk together in a bowl, put the flour into a second bowl and spread the breadcrumbs over a large plate. Dip the prawns into the flour, mayonnaise and then the breadcrumbs so that they take on an even coating. Treat them gently once they are done because the coating is quite delicate. Pick them up by their tails, drop them into the hot oil, about 6 at a time, and fry for 1 minute, until crisp and golden. Transfer to a tray lined with kitchen paper and keep warm in a low oven while you cook the rest.

To serve, spread the bottom half of each piece of bread with a little of the mayonnaise, then put some lettuce leaves on top. Pile on a few of the fried prawns, cover with the top halves of the bread and eat straight away.

tiger prawn and avocado salad

We are lucky enough to be endowed with our own native prawns in this country, which are delightfully delicate in flavour, if a little on the small side – but we can also very easily buy the best meaty, firm prawns from literally all over the world.

SERVES 4

1 LARGE AVOCADO

1 TEASPOON LIME JUICE

350 G (12 OZ) LARGE COOKED PEELED TIGER PRAWNS

1 TEASPOON THAI FISH SAUCE (*NAM PLA*)

2 TABLESPOONS FINELY SHREDDED MINT LEAVES

4 SPRING ONIONS, TRIMMED, HALVED AND FINELY SHREDDED LENGTHWAYS

100 G (4 OZ) FRESH BEANSPROUTS

50 G (2 OZ) WATERCRESS SPRIGS

4 TEASPOONS DARK SOY SAUCE

½ TEASPOON ROASTED SESAME OIL

1 TEASPOON CASTER SUGAR

2 TABLESPOONS VERY SMALL MINT LEAVES, TO GARNISH

SALT

METHOD

Cut the avocado in half and remove the stone. Halve again, then carefully peel off the skin and cut the flesh lengthways into long thin slices. Toss gently in a bowl with the lime juice and a pinch of salt.

Toss the prawns in another bowl with the fish sauce and shredded mint. Arrange the avocado slices, prawns, spring onions, beansprouts and watercress on 4 cold plates.

Whisk together the soy sauce, 4 teaspoons of cold water, sesame oil and caster sugar. Drizzle over the salad and then scatter with the small mint leaves. Serve immediately.

deep-fried prawn wontons with chilli jam

Here, the prawns are enclosed in wonton wrappers but the tails are left on and, to highlight the appearance, are not wrapped, otherwise they look a bit like Egyptian mummies. They are served with a dark chilli and onion relish flavoured with garlic, ginger and soy sauce. Large raw prawns in the shell are now available at most supermarkets and wonton wrappers can be bought in oriental food shops. Try to use Chinese rather than Japanese wrappers as they puff up nicely during frying.

SERVES 4

20 RAW UNSHELLED PRAWNS, HEADS REMOVED (SEE P. 7)

20 CHINESE WONTON WRAPPERS

OIL, FOR DEEP-FRYING

FOR THE CHILLI JAM:

50 ML (2 FL OZ) SUNFLOWER OIL OR VEGETABLE OIL

15 G (½ OZ) GARLIC CLOVES, VERY FINELY CHOPPED

15 G (½ OZ) FRESH ROOT GINGER, VERY FINELY CHOPPED

225 G (8 OZ) ONIONS, VERY FINELY CHOPPED

5 LARGE RED FINGER CHILLIES, SEEDED AND VERY FINELY CHOPPED

100 ML (3½ FL OZ) RED WINE VINEGAR

25 ML (1 FL OZ) JAPANESE SOY SAUCE

½ TEASPOON GROUND STAR ANISE

15 G (½ OZ) PALM SUGAR OR LIGHT MUSCOVADO SUGAR

SALT

METHOD

Peel the prawns, leaving the last tail segment in place (see p. 7) and reserve the shells. Heat the oil for the chilli jam in a medium-sized pan, add the shells and fry over a high heat for 1–2 minutes, until they are quite crisp. Tip everything into a sieve resting over a small pan and press really well to remove all the oil. The oil will now be pleasantly flavoured with prawn.

For the chilli jam, reheat the oil, add the garlic and ginger and fry quickly until both are beginning to colour. Add the onions and chillies and fry fiercely for 3–4 minutes. Stir in the vinegar, soy sauce, star anise, sugar and some salt to taste. Bring to the boil and simmer gently for 20–30 minutes, until the onions are very soft and the jam is well reduced and thick. Leave to cool, then spoon into 4 small dipping bowls or ramekins.

Wrap each prawn in 1 of the wonton wrappers, leaving the tail end uncovered, and seal with a little water. Pour the oil into a pan until it is about one-third full. Heat to 190°C/375°F or until a small piece of white bread dropped in the oil browns and rises to the surface in 1 minute. Fry the prawns in batches for about 1–1½ minutes, until crisp and golden. Lift out and drain briefly on kitchen paper. Serve hot with the chilli jam.

stir-fried prawns

This is a Szechuan recipe often characterized by plenty of chilli. The chilli bean sauce in the recipe can be easily bought at Chinese supermarkets but, if you can't get hold of it, mix together yellow bean sauce and chilli sauce. If you want to make the dish even hotter, put in a few finely chopped red chillies as well.

SERVES 4

1 TEASPOON SZECHUAN PEPPERCORNS

½ TEASPOON BLACK PEPPERCORNS

1 TABLESPOON GROUNDNUT OIL

3 SPRING ONIONS, WHITE AND GREEN SEPARATED, FINELY SLICED

2.5 CM (1 IN) FRESH ROOT GINGER, FINELY CHOPPED

4 GARLIC CLOVES, FINELY CHOPPED

450 G (1 LB) RAW PEELED PRAWNS

1 TEASPOON DRY SHERRY

1 TABLESPOON SOY SAUCE

2 TABLESPOONS CHILLI BEAN SAUCE

225 G (8 OZ) TOMATOES, SKINNED AND SLICED

½ TEASPOON SUGAR

METHOD

Grind together the Szechuan and black peppercorns. Put the groundnut oil in a wok or a large frying pan and stir-fry the white part of the spring onions, the ginger and the garlic for 1 minute. Add the prawns and the ground peppercorns and stir-fry for another minute, then add the sherry, soy sauce, chilli bean sauce, tomatoes and sugar. Cover and cook for 3 minutes. Sprinkle with the green part of the spring onions and serve.

north atlantic prawn pilaf

Like a number of recipes in this book, this uses ingredients you can get from any fishmonger or supermarket. I really want this book to be used every day. This is a nice, gentle dish, ideal for supper with a glass of New Zealand Chardonnay.

SERVES 4

800 G (1 LB 12 OZ) COOKED UNSHELLED NORTH ATLANTIC PRAWNS

50 G (2 OZ) BUTTER

1 SMALL ONION, CHOPPED

1 SMALL CARROT, ROUGHLY CHOPPED

½ TEASPOON TOMATO PURÉE

900 ML (1½ PINTS) *CHICKEN STOCK* (SEE P. 140)

2 SHALLOTS, FINELY CHOPPED

1 GARLIC CLOVE, VERY FINELY CHOPPED

3 CLOVES

3 GREEN CARDAMOM PODS

1 CINNAMON STICK, BROKEN INTO 4 PIECES

¼ TEASPOON TURMERIC POWDER

275 G (10 OZ) BASMATI RICE

3 TABLESPOONS CHOPPED CORIANDER

3 PLUM TOMATOES, SKINNED, SEEDED AND DICED

SALT AND FRESHLY GROUND BLACK PEPPER

METHOD

Peel the prawns (see p. 7) but keep the heads and shells. Put the prawns on a plate and set aside. Heat 25 g (1 oz) of the butter in a large pan, add the onion and carrot and fry over a medium heat for 6–7 minutes, until lightly browned. Add the prawn heads and shells and continue to fry for 3–4 minutes. Add the tomato purée and chicken stock, bring to the boil and simmer for 15 minutes. Strain into a measuring jug; if there is more than 600 ml (1 pint), return to the pan and boil rapidly until reduced to this amount.

Melt the rest of the butter in a pan and add the shallots, garlic, cloves, cardamom pods, cinnamon pieces and turmeric and fry gently for 5 minutes. Add the rice and stir well to coat with the spicy butter. Add the stock to the pan, season with salt and bring to the boil, then turn the heat right down to the slightest simmer, put a lid on the pan and leave to simmer for 15 minutes. Don't lift the lid during this time.

Uncover and gently stir in the peeled prawns, coriander, diced tomatoes and salt and pepper to taste. Re-cover and leave for 5 minutes to warm through. Then spoon into a warmed serving dish and serve.

prawn caldine

This is one of the best dishes I cooked when I was filming in India for my series *Rick Stein's Seafood Odyssey*. Unusually for a Goan seafood dish, it is particularly light and fragrant, with distinctive little wisps of green chilli in the sauce. We found a spot under some banyan trees in which to film. This overlooked a wide estuary where the locals were picking clams – some commercially, others just out on a Sunday excursion. We named the spot 'Clam Pickers' Bluff' and spent much of the day trying to dislodge particularly noisy crows from the trees by hurling stones at them. It was pretty unsuccessful, and they finally made off with the last of the finished *caldine*. The director has now called for a catapult to be part of the crew's kit when we next have to film in India.

SERVES 4

550 G (1¼ LB) RAW UNSHELLED PRAWNS, HEADS REMOVED

2 TABLESPOONS COCONUT VINEGAR OR WHITE WINE VINEGAR

1 TEASPOON TURMERIC POWDER

1 TEASPOON BLACK PEPPERCORNS

1 TABLESPOON CORIANDER SEEDS

1 TEASPOON CUMIN SEEDS

2 TABLESPOONS WHITE POPPY SEEDS OR GROUND ALMONDS

4 TABLESPOONS GROUNDNUT OIL

1 ONION, THINLY SLICED

3 GARLIC CLOVES, CUT INTO SLIVERS

2.5 CM (1 IN) FRESH ROOT GINGER, FINELY CHOPPED

400 ML (14 FL OZ) COCONUT MILK

4 TABLESPOONS *TAMARIND WATER* (SEE P. 142)

5 MILD GREEN FINGER CHILLIES, HALVED, SEEDED AND CUT INTO LONG, THIN SHREDS

2 TABLESPOONS CHOPPED CORIANDER

SALT

METHOD

Peel the prawns, leaving the last tail segment in place (see p. 7). Mix the prawns with the vinegar and ½ teaspoon of salt and leave for 5 minutes or so. This enhances the flavour. Meanwhile, put the turmeric, peppercorns, coriander seeds, cumin seeds and white poppy seeds, if using, into a spice grinder and grind to a fine powder.

Heat the oil in a medium-sized pan. Add the onion, garlic and ginger and fry gently for 5 minutes. Stir in the ground spices and fry for 2 minutes. Add the ground almonds if you aren't using poppy seeds, plus the coconut milk, tamarind water, 150 ml (5 fl oz) of water, three-quarters of the sliced chillies and ½ teaspoon of salt. Bring to a simmer and cook for 5 minutes. Add the prawns and simmer for only 3–4 minutes so they don't overcook. Stir in the rest of the sliced chillies and the coriander and serve with some steamed basmati rice.

tandoori prawns

The tandoori spice mix that I use for my prawns is quite unconventional. Although it includes all the standard tandoori marinade ingredients, such as yoghurt, lemon juice, chilli and curry spices, I also put in a great deal of pounded fennel seed, which I find gives the marinated prawns an incomparable texture and aromatic flavour. Do splash out on the best-possible whole uncooked prawns for this dish; it is well worth it.

SERVES 4

32 LARGE RAW UNSHELLED PRAWNS

175 G (6 OZ) GREEK-STYLE NATURAL YOGHURT

1 QUANTITY *KACHUMBER SALAD* (SEE P. 140), TO SERVE

FOR THE LEMON CHILLI MARINADE:

1 TEASPOON CAYENNE PEPPER

1 TEASPOON SALT

JUICE OF 1 LEMON

FOR THE TANDOORI MASALA PASTE:

15 G (½ OZ) FENNEL SEEDS

1 TABLESPOON CORIANDER SEEDS

1 TABLESPOON CUMIN SEEDS

25 G (1 OZ) FRESH ROOT GINGER, ROUGHLY CHOPPED

6 GARLIC CLOVES, CHOPPED

4 MEDIUM-HOT RED DUTCH CHILLIES, SEEDED AND ROUGHLY CHOPPED

2 TEASPOONS PAPRIKA

1 TEASPOON TURMERIC POWDER

JUICE OF 1 LEMON

METHOD

If you are cooking the prawns on the barbecue, light it now. Mix together the ingredients for the lemon chilli marinade. Make 3 small slits in either side of each prawn, between the shell segments, to allow the marinade to penetrate. Put the prawns and marinade into a bowl, toss together and set aside for 20 minutes.

For the tandoori masala paste, put the fennel seeds, coriander seeds and cumin seeds together in a spice grinder or mortar and grind to a fine powder. Tip the spices into a food processor, add the rest of the masala paste ingredients and blend until smooth. Stir the paste into the yoghurt and then stir this into the prawns. Leave for another 20 minutes.

If you are cooking the prawns under the grill, pre-heat the grill to high. Thread the prawns on to metal or soaked bamboo skewers, piercing them just behind the head and through the tail. Cook them on the barbecue or under a very hot grill for 2 minutes on each side.

While the prawns are cooking, layer the ingredients for the salad in a shallow dish. Serve the prawns with the salad and maybe some warm naan bread.

stir-fried salt and pepper prawns

The idea for this recipe came from a dish I had on Lamma Island, Hong Kong, where I was struck by the starkness of the accompaniments – just salt and pepper. Actually, there is a bit more to it than that. I finally tracked down a recipe in Yan-Kit So's *Classic Chinese Cookbook*, so here it is.

SERVES 4

2 TABLESPOONS SALT

1 TEASPOON CHINESE FIVE-SPICE POWDER

1 TEASPOON GROUND SZECHUAN PEPPERCORNS

1 TEASPOON GROUND BLACK PEPPER

SUNFLOWER OIL, FOR DEEP-FRYING

900 G (2 LB) RAW UNSHELLED PRAWNS, HEADS REMOVED (SEE P. 7)

METHOD

Heat a dry wok or a large frying pan over a medium heat. Add the salt and stir constantly for about 4 minutes, until it has turned a slightly greyish colour. Transfer to a small bowl and mix with the five-spice powder, Szechuan pepper and black pepper.

Pour some oil into a large pan until it is about one-third full and heat to 180°C/350°F or until a small piece of white bread dropped into the oil browns and rises to the surface in 1 minute. Add half the prawns and fry for 30 seconds, until they have curled up and turned pink. Remove and repeat with the remaining prawns.

Reheat the dry wok or frying pan, add 2 tablespoons of the spiced salt and the cooked prawns, then flip the prawns over in the salt for 30 seconds so that it can permeate them. Tip on to warm serving plates and serve the remaining salt separately.

pad thai noodles with prawns

This dish, which every Thai restaurant has on its menu, almost doesn't have a proper recipe, it varies so much from place to place. Sometimes it comes out luminous orange, sometimes it's very wet, sometimes too dry, others are disgustingly sweet and on some occasions it's far too hot. I must have eaten about ten versions while trying to track down the perfect recipe, including five in Thailand, but I finally found the best one in south London, of all places, at the Pepper Tree restaurant on Clapham Common. I think that it should be sweet but not too sweet, tart but not too tart and dry but not too dry. And above all, the noodles should still have a little bit of bite to them just like pasta, and some beansprouts and spring onions should be thrown on top at the last minute. Then you're in danger of falling into an eating frenzy.

SERVES 2

175 G (6 OZ) FLAT RICE NOODLES

50 ML (2 FL OZ) GROUNDNUT OIL

2 GARLIC CLOVES, FINELY CHOPPED

½ TEASPOON DRIED CHILLI FLAKES

10 LARGE RAW PEELED PRAWNS

2 EGGS, BEATEN

2–3 TABLESPOONS THAI FISH SAUCE (*NAM PLA*)

2–3 TABLESPOONS *TAMARIND WATER* (SEE P. 142)

1 TABLESPOON PALM SUGAR OR LIGHT MUSCOVADO SUGAR

1 TABLESPOON DRIED SHRIMPS, COARSELY CHOPPED

4 HEAPED TABLESPOONS ROASTED PEANUTS, COARSELY CHOPPED

4 SPRING ONIONS, CUT INTO 5 CM (2 IN) PIECES AND FINELY
    SHREDDED LENGTHWAYS

50 G (2 OZ) FRESH BEANSPROUTS

2 TABLESPOONS ROUGHLY CHOPPED CORIANDER

METHOD

Soak the noodles in cold water for 1 hour, then drain and set to one side.

Heat the oil in a wok or a large frying pan over a high heat. Add the garlic, chilli flakes and prawns and stir-fry for 2–3 minutes, until the prawns are just cooked.

Pour in the beaten eggs and stir-fry for a few seconds, until they just start to look scrambled. Lower the heat, add the noodles, fish sauce, tamarind water and sugar and toss together for a minute or two until the noodles are tender.

Add the dried shrimps, half the peanuts, half the spring onions, half the beansprouts and all the coriander and toss for another minute. Serve sprinkled with the rest of the peanuts, spring onions and beansprouts.

grilled dublin bay prawns with
a pernod and olive oil dressing

I got the sauce for this from re-reading Elizabeth David's *An Omelette and a Glass of Wine*. Some recipes just jump off the page at you as essential to do now – this is particularly common with recipes from Elizabeth David's books. It's the sort of sauce I would love to have invented for all members of the lobster family. The combination of the aniseed flavours of the Pernod and tarragon, salted with a little soy and sharpened with lemon juice, serves to 'tease you out of thought', as Keats might have said. You could substitute two 450 g (1 lb) cooked lobsters for the Dublin Bay prawns, serving half a lobster per person, if you wish.

SERVES 4

16 LARGE OR 24 SMALLER COOKED DUBLIN BAY PRAWNS (LANGOUSTINES)

2 SMALL SHALLOTS, FINELY CHOPPED

½ TABLESPOON ROUGHLY CHOPPED TARRAGON

½ TABLESPOON ROUGHLY CHOPPED FLAT-LEAF PARSLEY

1 TEASPOON DIJON MUSTARD

1 TEASPOON DARK SOY SAUCE

85 ML (3 FL OZ) EXTRA VIRGIN OLIVE OIL

1½ TABLESPOONS FRESH LEMON JUICE

1 TEASPOON PERNOD

50 G (2 OZ) BUTTER, MELTED

SALT AND FRESHLY GROUND BLACK PEPPER

METHOD

Pre-heat the grill to high. Cut the Dublin Bay prawns open lengthways and scoop out the creamy contents of the heads and any red roe with a teaspoon. Put this into a small bowl and stir in the shallots, tarragon, parsley, mustard, soy sauce, oil, lemon juice, Pernod and a little salt and pepper to taste.

Place the halved prawns cut-side up on a baking tray or the rack of the grill pan and brush with the melted butter. Season lightly and grill for 2–3 minutes, until the shells as well as the meat are heated through. Put the prawns on 4 serving plates and spoon over a little of the dressing. Divide the rest of the dressing between 4 dipping saucers or small ramekins and serve.

prawn-stuffed papads

Like so many of my Goan recipes, this comes from Rui Madre de Deus, at the Ronil Beach Resort Hotel in Baga. It makes the most delightful appetizer and is ideal as a nicely spicy canapé for a drinks party. You have to be a bit careful with the *papads*, or poppadoms, though. When we were making them in India we found that it's easy enough to buy freshly made poppadoms there that are quite flexible, but in the UK you need to buy a good brand. Try to get them from an Indian grocer because they will be slightly bendy (and far cheaper than the supermarket boxed ones). Liberally brush them with water, then leave them for a couple of minutes until they are moist enough to fold. This recipe can make as many as 48 pieces, depending on the number of poppadoms you use.

MAKES 42

2 TABLESPOONS GROUNDNUT OIL OR SUNFLOWER OIL, PLUS EXTRA
   FOR SHALLOW-FRYING

225 G (8 OZ) ONIONS, FINELY CHOPPED

225 G (8 OZ) TOMATOES, SKINNED AND CHOPPED

275 G (10 OZ) RAW PEELED PRAWNS, FINELY CHOPPED

3–4 GREEN FINGER CHILLIES, SEEDED AND FINELY CHOPPED

2 GARLIC CLOVES, CRUSHED

2.5 CM (1 IN) FRESH ROOT GINGER, FINELY GRATED

1 TEASPOON TURMERIC POWDER

1 TEASPOON CHILLI POWDER

JUICE OF ½ LIME

½ TEASPOON SALT

14–16 x 15 CM (6 IN) UNCOOKED PLAIN POPPADAMS

1 SMALL EGG, BEATEN

METHOD

Heat the 2 tablespoons of oil in a frying pan, add the onions and fry over a high heat, stirring now and then, until they are richly golden. Add the tomatoes and continue to fry until everything has reduced down to a golden-coloured paste. Add the chopped prawns, chillies, garlic, ginger, turmeric, chilli powder, lime juice and salt. Fry for about 1 minute, until the prawns are cooked, then take off the heat.

Pour about 5 mm (¼ in) of oil into another frying pan and heat it to 200°C/400°F. Taking 2–3 poppadoms at a time, brush them generously with water on both sides and leave to soften for 2 minutes. Place 2 good tablespoons of the prawn filling down the centre of each one and brush the edge with a little beaten egg. Roll them up and press the open ends together to seal.

Once you have filled all the *papads*, shallow-fry them 3 or 4 at a time for 1–1½ minutes, turning them frequently, until crisp and golden. Place on kitchen paper to remove any greasiness, then slice off the ends and cut each one into 3 pieces. Spear each piece with a cocktail stick and serve hot.

gremolata prawns

Gremolata is what I call the traditional equivalent to the French *persillade*, which is parsley finely chopped with garlic. I included a recipe in my book *Taste of the Sea* for deep-fried whitebait with *persillade* and now it's the turn of the prawn, with just a pinch of cayenne pepper to liven things up. I love eating seafood with my fingers, which is why I've left the shells on the prawns. As you split open the shells, the *gremolata* will flavour the flesh.

SERVES 4

1 LARGE LEMON

2 TABLESPOONS OLIVE OIL

20 LARGE RAW UNSHELLED PRAWNS

CAYENNE PEPPER (OPTIONAL)

3 GARLIC CLOVES, VERY FINELY CHOPPED

4 TABLESPOONS CHOPPED FLAT-LEAF PARSLEY

COARSE SEA SALT AND FRESHLY GROUND BLACK PEPPER

METHOD

Peel the zest off the lemon with a potato peeler, pile the pieces up a few at a time and then cut them across into short, thin strips. Heat the oil in a large frying pan. Add the prawns and toss them over a high heat for 4–5 minutes, seasoning them with some cayenne pepper or black pepper and salt as you do so.

Cut the lemon in half and squeeze the juice from one half over the prawns. Continue to cook until the juice has almost evaporated – the prawns should be quite dry. Take the pan off the heat and leave for about 1 minute to cool very slightly. Then sprinkle over the lemon zest, chopped garlic, parsley and ¼ teaspoon of salt and toss together well. Pile the prawns into a large serving dish and serve with some finger bowls and plenty of napkins.

prawn jambalaya

Jambalaya comes from New Orleans and is based on paella but not being able to get saffron and olive oil the Spanish settlers used what was available locally and in using the combination of green peppers, celery and onions they produced what is now known as the 'holy trinity', the flavour that most typifies Creole cookery.

Raw prawn tails are now available in most supermarkets. For extra flavour in the jambalaya, fry the shells in about 50 ml (2 fl oz) of vegetable oil then pass the oil through a sieve into the dish just before adding the rice.

SERVES 6

4 TABLESPOONS SUNFLOWER OIL

100 G (4 OZ) CHORIZO OR SPICY SMOKED SAUSAGE, SLICED

2 TEASPOONS PAPRIKA

8 GARLIC CLOVES, CHOPPED

1 MEDIUM ONION, CHOPPED

2 GREEN PEPPERS, SEEDED AND CHOPPED

4 CELERY STICKS, SLICED

2 MEDIUM-HOT RED DUTCH CHILLIES, SEEDED AND FINELY CHOPPED

450 G (1 LB) SKINNED BONELESS CHICKEN, CUT INTO 2.5 CM (1 IN) PIECES

450 G (1 LB) RAW PEELED PRAWNS, HEADS REMOVED (SEE P. 7)

2 BAY LEAVES

LEAVES FROM A SPRIG OF THYME

1 TEASPOON CHOPPED OREGANO

450 G (1 LB) LONG-GRAIN RICE

1.2 LITRES (2 PINTS) *CHICKEN STOCK* (SEE P. 140)

3 SPRING ONIONS, TRIMMED AND THINLY SLICED

SALT AND CAYENNE PEPPER

METHOD

Heat the oil in a large deep frying pan. Add the sliced sausage and fry until lightly browned. Add the paprika and stir to colour the oil.

Add the garlic, cook for 30 seconds, and then add the onion, green peppers, celery and chillies. Cook over a medium heat until lightly browned.

Add the chicken, prawns, bay leaves, thyme and oregano and fry over a medium heat for 5 minutes.

Add the rice and stir for 2 minutes. Add the chicken stock and 1 teaspoon of salt, bring to the boil, cover and simmer for about 15 minutes, until the rice has absorbed all the liquid and is tender.

Stir in the spring onions and some cayenne pepper to taste. Serve with a green salad.

paper-wrapped prawns in honey and ginger

This is a delightful, easy little appetite stimulator, the sort of thing you might serve up with a few ice-cold bottles of Tiger beer. Keeping the ingredients to a minimum does nothing to diminish the excitement of the taste when you open up these little deep-fried parcels.

SERVES 4

32 LARGE RAW PEELED PRAWNS

5 CM (2 IN) FRESH ROOT GINGER, UNPEELED

2 TABLESPOONS CLEAR HONEY

2 TABLESPOONS CHINESE RICE WINE OR DRY SHERRY

2 TABLESPOONS DARK SOY SAUCE

6 SPRING ONIONS, THINLY SLICED

1 TEASPOON GROUND SZECHUAN PEPPERCORNS

SUNFLOWER OIL, FOR DEEP-FRYING

METHOD

Place the prawns in a bowl. Finely grate the piece of root ginger on to a plate. Collect it all up and squeeze out the juice into the bowl containing the prawns, then stir in the honey, rice wine or sherry and soy sauce. Cover and leave to marinate in the fridge for 1 hour.

Cut out sixteen 18 cm (7 in) squares of non-stick baking paper. Put a square of paper on a work surface with a corner pointing towards you. Place 2 prawns in the centre and sprinkle over a few of the chopped spring onions and some of the ground Szechuan pepper. Fold the corner nearest you into the centre of the square so that it just covers the prawns. Next fold over the left-hand corner, then the right-hand one. Fold the parcel in half and then tuck in the flap. Repeat with the rest of the paper squares and prawns.

Heat some oil for deep-frying to 190°C/375°F or until a small piece of white bread dropped into the oil browns and rises to the surface in 1 minute. Fry the parcels a few at a time for about 2 minutes. Remove with a slotted spoon, place on a tray lined with kitchen paper and leave to drain while you cook the rest. Serve immediately, letting your guests unwrap their own packages.

fritto misto di mare

This is my version of the classic Italian dish where small pieces of seafood are tossed in seasoned flour, then deep-fried in olive oil. Much as I've enjoyed this dish on many occasions, I've always baulked at putting it in a recipe book because of the high price of olive oil – there's no point in writing recipes if you have a suspicion that nobody is ever going to cook them. However, I spent some time trying to work out the minimum amount of oil you'd need to deep-fry four portions of this superb dish successfully, and I now present my own version of fritto misto, specially adapted to use just one bottle of olive oil.

SERVES 4

8 PREPARED SCALLOPS (SEE P. 8)

100 G (4 OZ) PREPARED SQUID (SEE P. 8)

12 LARGE RAW PRAWNS, PEELED AND HEADS REMOVED (SEE P. 7)

1 LITRE (1¾ PINTS) OLIVE OIL, FOR DEEP-FRYING

75 G (3 OZ) PLAIN FLOUR, SEASONED WITH SALT AND PEPPER

SALT

2 LEMON WEDGES

METHOD

Pre-heat the oven to 150°C/300°F/Gas 2. Line a large baking tray with plenty of kitchen paper.

Detach the coral from each scallop and slice it in half lengthways (this prevents it from exploding during cooking). Slice the scallop meat horizontally in half as well. Cut the squid across into thick rings. Season the scallops, squid and prawns with a little salt.

Pour the oil into a large pan and heat to 190°C/375°F or until a small piece of white bread dropped into the oil browns and rises to the surface in 1 minute. Toss the seafood in the seasoned flour and deep-fry a batch for 30 seconds–1 minute, until the floury coating is just beginning to be tinged with brown. Using a slotted spoon, lift out and place on the baking tray and keep hot in the oven while you cook the remainder. Serve with lemon wedges.

chargrilled tiger prawns with
lemongrass, chilli and coriander

Tiger prawns are now being farmed in large quantities in Thailand. They are easy to buy here and you should be able to get all the ingredients to make this first course at most large supermarkets or an oriental food shop. The dish is best cooked on a barbecue, but can also be cooked successfully under the grill, if you prefer.

SERVES 4

20 RAW UNSHELLED TIGER PRAWNS OR KING PRAWNS, EACH WEIGHING
ABOUT 25 G (1 OZ), HEADS REMOVED (SEE P. 7)
25 ML (1 FL OZ) GROUNDNUT OIL, SEASONED WITH 1 TEASPOON SALT AND
FRESHLY GROUND BLACK PEPPER

FOR THE DRESSING:
25 ML (1 FL OZ) THAI FISH SAUCE (*NAM PLA*)
1 MILD GREEN DUTCH CHILLI, SEEDED AND FINELY CHOPPED
1 LEMONGRASS STALK, OUTER LEAVES REMOVED AND THE CORE FINELY SLICED
JUICE OF 1 LEMON
½ TEASPOON SUGAR

FOR THE SALAD:
A SMALL BUNCH OF CORIANDER
½ ICEBERG LETTUCE, FINELY SLICED

METHOD

Light the barbecue at least 30 minutes before you want to start cooking. The secret of successful barbecuing lies in getting the grill bar so hot that anything you put on it sears and carbonizes quickly and so doesn't stick. If you are using bamboo skewers, soak them in cold water for 30 minutes to stop them from catching light on the barbecue or under the grill.

Remove the shells from the prawns, except for the last small piece on the end of the tail (see p. 7). Cut the bodies in half lengthways, leaving them joined at the tail. Using a pastry brush, paint the prawns liberally with the seasoned oil. Thread 5 prawns on to each skewer and set aside until needed.

For the dressing, in a bowl mix together the fish sauce, 150 ml (5 fl oz) of water and the chilli. Add the lemongrass to the dressing with the lemon juice and sugar.

Pick off about 20 of the best coriander leaves to use in the salad and reserve. Chop the remainder finely and set aside.

Pre-heat the grill to high, if using, and barbecue or grill the prawns for exactly 5 minutes, turning them half-way through the cooking time. Warm the dressing over a gentle heat and add the chopped coriander to the pan just before taking it off the heat. Place the whole coriander leaves and lettuce on 4 warmed plates, top with the skewered prawns and spoon over the dressing.

sautéed scallops with basil, saffron and pasta

Scallop shells make excellent containers for seafood. You will need 20 scallop shells for this recipe. If it is possible, buy the scallops and shells together, though you will need to buy extra empty shells as well.

SERVES 4

12 GOOD-SIZED PREPARED SCALLOPS (SEE P. 8)

600 ML (1 PINT) *FISH STOCK* (SEE P. 140)

50 ML (2 FL OZ) WHITE WINE

A GOOD PINCH OF SAFFRON

150 ML (5 FL OZ) DOUBLE CREAM

50 G (2 OZ) UNSALTED BUTTER, PLUS EXTRA FOR THE PASTA

100 G (4 OZ) THIN PASTA SUCH AS VERMICELLI OR *FEDILINI*

6 BASIL LEAVES, SLICED

METHOD

Slice the scallops in half horizontally. Put the fish stock, white wine and saffron in a pan and boil rapidly to reduce by three-quarters. Add the cream and butter and reduce further until the sauce coats the back of a spoon.

Boil the pasta in salted water until tender but firm to the bite (*al dente*). Toss in a little butter with the sliced basil leaves.

Warm the 20 scallop shells under a moderate grill and arrange on 4 warmed plates. Distribute the pasta between the shells and bring the sauce to the boil. Add the sliced scallops and cook for 2 minutes. Spoon the scallops and sauce into the shells and serve.

steamed scallops in the shell with
ginger, soy, sesame oil and spring onions

This recipe came to me as a result of a visit to a restaurant in Gerrard Street, Soho. It is fascinating to me how the Chinese restaurants in London's Soho have grown in everyone's estimation in the last thirty-odd years. I can recall in the early days seeing dark red ducks hanging in every front window and wondering how anyone except the Chinese would dare to eat such frightening-looking food. The smell was enough to scare you rigid and the look of the stuff – wow! Then about twenty-five years ago I went with a more adventurous friend to the Lido in Gerrard Street. He said I should try anything, it would all be good. So I ordered the most dreadful-sounding dishes on the menu, *Boiled Eel in Black Bean Sauce* and, I think, *Steamed Fish Heads*. It was all totally wonderful and I've been back many times since.

SERVES 4

16 PREPARED SCALLOPS IN THEIR SHELLS (SEE P. 8)

1 TEASPOON FINELY CHOPPED FRESH ROOT GINGER

1 TABLESPOON SESAME OIL

2 TABLESPOONS DARK SOY SAUCE

1 TABLESPOON ROUGHLY CHOPPED CORIANDER

3 SPRING ONIONS, THINLY SLICED

METHOD

Pour 2.5 cm (1 in) of water into the base of a wide, shallow pan and bring it to the boil. Loosen the scallops from their shells but leave them in place. Sprinkle each one with some of the ginger.

Arrange the scallops, in batches if necessary, on a petal steamer. Lower them into the pan, reduce the heat to medium, cover and cook for about 4 minutes until just set. Remove and keep warm while you cook the rest.

Meanwhile, put the sesame oil and soy sauce into a small pan and warm through.

Lift the scallops on to 4 warmed plates and pour over some of the warm soy sauce and sesame oil. Sprinkle over the coriander and spring onions and serve immediately.

seared scallops with ibérico ham

Ibérico ham is the best cured ham in Spain. It is taken from the *Ibérico negro* pig, which is allowed to run free in the oak forests, getting plenty of exercise and therefore staying lean. It is very similar to the Italian Parma or French Bayonne ham but it has its own distinctive and very fine flavour. However, you can use any cured or air-dried ham in its place if you wish. The salad for this dish should be the hearts of frisée or curly endive lettuce. What I mean by that is the lovely, crisp blanched leaves from the centre of the lettuce that haven't turned green because of exposure to the light. It's a pity that British supermarkets only seem to sell them in bags of washed salad leaves. I love those massive heads of bitter, chicory-type leaves like *frisée de ruffec, escarole* or *cornet de Bordeaux* in France and similar whole salads in Italian and Spanish markets.

SERVES 4

8 THIN SLICES OF IBÉRICO HAM OR A SIMILAR CURED HAM

LEAVES FROM 1 FRISÉE LETTUCE HEART, PLUS A HANDFUL OF OTHER
   BITTER SALAD LEAVES

50 G (2 OZ) CHILLED UNSALTED BUTTER

12 PREPARED SCALLOPS (SEE P. 8)

3 TABLESPOONS SHERRY VINEGAR

1 TABLESPOON CHOPPED PARSLEY

SALT AND FRESHLY GROUND BLACK PEPPER

METHOD

Arrange the ham and a pile of the salad leaves on 4 plates. Generously rub the base of a large non-stick frying pan with the block of butter and cut the remainder into small pieces.

Set the pan over a high heat and, as soon as the butter starts to smoke, add the scallops and sear for 2 minutes on each side, seasoning them with a little salt and pepper as they cook. Arrange the scallops on top of the ham.

For the dressing, remove the pan from the heat, add the sherry vinegar and stir to scrape up any residue from the bottom of the pan. Return the pan to the heat and whisk in the pieces of butter, a few at a time, then add the parsley and season with a little salt and pepper. Spoon the dressing over the leaves and serve at once.

scallops with noisette butter

This is a simple recipe but *noisette* butter needs to be made correctly to taste really good. It goes very well with grilled or fried fillets of any flat fish and any number of the cod family like whiting, hake or haddock. If you are making this as a starter, it would be more appropriate to use queen scallops. Queens are a type of small scallop. The only difference between it and the larger bivalve is that it has two concave shells whereas the scallop has one concave and one flat shell.

SERVES 4

225 G (8 OZ) UNSALTED BUTTER

16 PREPARED SCALLOPS OR 24 PREPARED QUEEN SCALLOPS IN THEIR SHELLS
   (SEE P. 8)

JUICE OF ½ LEMON

A SMALL BUNCH OF PARSLEY

SALT AND FRESHLY GROUND BLACK PEPPER

METHOD

Pre-heat the grill to high.

Cut up the butter and place in a small pan. Set the pan over a medium heat until the butter has melted and started to brown. This is the important bit of the recipe – the butter needs to go a delicate but not dark shade of brown. The word *noisette* means nutty and that is how you can tell when it is cooked enough – when it smells of warm nuts. Remove from the heat as soon as the butter has reached that stage and keep warm.

Brush the scallops with a little of the *noisette* butter and grill for 5 minutes. Remove and place on 4 warmed plates. Squeeze over the lemon juice and season with salt and pepper. Pour the remaining *noisette* butter over all the scallops and scatter with the parsley.

Serve with plenty of fresh crusty bread to mop up the juices.

sautéed scallops with lentils and chardonnay

I use oaked Australian Chardonnay in large quantities for this dish, along with a pinch of spice normally associated with Indian cookery. You only need about an eighth of a teaspoon of spice to go into the sauce so I have had to specify the quantities as small pinches and large pinches.

SERVES 4

12 PREPARED SCALLOPS (SEE P. 8)

FOR THE SAUCE:
A SMALL PINCH OF GROUND ALLSPICE
A SMALL PINCH OF GROUND CLOVE
A SMALL PINCH OF GROUND NUTMEG
A LARGE PINCH OF CURRY POWDER
50 G (2 OZ) UNSALTED BUTTER, CUT INTO CUBES, PLUS 10 G (½ OZ)
25 G (1 OZ) ONION, CHOPPED
25 G (1 OZ) CARROT, CHOPPED
300 ML (10 FL OZ) OAKED CHARDONNAY
600 ML (1 PINT) *FISH STOCK* (SEE P. 140)
50 ML (2 FL OZ) DOUBLE CREAM

FOR THE LENTILS:
50 G (2 OZ) GREEN LENTILS, PREFERABLY PUY LENTILS
175 ML (6 FL OZ) *FISH STOCK* (SEE P. 140)
1 CLOVE
1 BAY LEAF
2 SLICES OF ONION
½ TEASPOON SALT

METHOD

For the sauce, put the spices, 10 g (½ oz) of butter, the onion and carrot in a pan and cook over a gentle heat for about 4 minutes. Pour in the Chardonnay and fish stock and bring to the boil. Simmer until the volume has reduced by about two-thirds. Strain the stock, add the cream and simmer again until the volume has reduced by about two-thirds. While the sauce is reducing, simmer the lentils with the fish stock, clove, bay leaf, onion and salt until tender. Drain.

Detach the corals and cut each scallop horizontally into 3 discs. Put a frying pan over a high heat. When hot, rub a little of the cubed butter over the pan then put in half the scallop slices and corals. Cook for 40 seconds only on one side to caramelize, then turn and cook for a further 30 seconds on the other.

Remove and keep warm. Pour any juices into the sauce. Heat the pan again, add a little more butter and fry the second batch of scallop slices and corals.

Place a pile of lentils on each of 4 warmed plates and arrange the scallops and corals on top. Whisk the remaining cubes of butter into the warm sauce and pour round each plate.

scallops with duck livers and spaghettini

This dish is designed to be cooked at the last minute, so you need to be well prepared beforehand. It is most successful if you can use fresh duck livers. These are hard to get hold of, however, and you will probably have to make do with frozen ones. You need to be careful with frozen livers because if they've been frozen for too long they tend to go soft and don't plump up nicely during cooking. Freshly frozen ones should be bright red – the older they are, the greyer they become. A perfect wine to go with this would be a chilled Gewürztraminer or a Tokay Pinot Gris from Alsace.

SERVES 4

12 LARGE PREPARED SCALLOPS (SEE P. 8)

100 G (4 OZ) DUCK LIVERS

300 ML (10 FL OZ) *FISH STOCK* (SEE P. 140)

120 ML (4 FL OZ) DOUBLE CREAM

120 ML (4 FL OZ) MUSCAT DE BEAUMES DE VENISE OR
  A SIMILAR SWEET WHITE WINE

175 G (6 OZ) DRIED SPAGHETTINI

25 G (1 OZ) UNSALTED BUTTER

SALT AND FRESHLY GROUND BLACK PEPPER

SPRIGS OF FLAT-LEAF PARSLEY, TO GARNISH

METHOD

Bring a large pan of well-salted water (i.e. 1 teaspoon per 600 ml/1 pint) to the boil. Meanwhile, slice the scallops horizontally in half and cut the duck livers into similar-sized pieces, being sure to remove any traces of the greeny-yellow gall bladder.

Put the fish stock, 85 ml (3 fl oz) of the cream and the wine into a wide-based pan and boil rapidly until reduced to 150 ml (5 fl oz).

Add the pasta to the pan of boiling water and cook for 4 minutes or until *al dente*. Drain, then cover and keep warm.

Melt a small knob of the butter in a frying pan over a high heat. Add the scallop slices and fry them for 30 seconds on each side. Transfer them to a plate and keep warm.

Add the rest of the butter to the frying pan with the duck livers and fry for just 1 minute, turning them over as they colour. Set aside with the scallops.

Add the reduced stock and wine mixture to the frying pan and bring to the boil, scraping up all the bits from the bottom of the pan. Strain through a sieve into a small pan, stir in the rest of the cream, check the seasoning and heat through.

To serve, pile the pasta on to 4 warmed plates and arrange the scallops and duck livers on top. Pour the sauce around the pasta and serve garnished with sprigs of parsley.

seared scallop salad with parma ham and croûtons

A simple salad of young leaves with scallops, strips of Parma ham and granary bread croûtons, finished with a few snipped chives. The scallops are sautéed in a hot frying pan in which a very small amount of butter has been melted, giving them a really sweet, caramelized exterior. But they are only cooked briefly so that they remain succulent.

SERVES 4

12 PREPARED SCALLOPS OR 24 PREPARED QUEEN SCALLOPS (SEE P. 8)

35 G (1¼ OZ) UNSALTED BUTTER

3 SLICES OF GRANARY BREAD, 1 CM (½ IN) THICK, CRUSTS REMOVED, CUT INTO 1 CM (½ IN) CUBES

100 G (4 OZ) BAG OF MIXED BABY LEAF SALAD

8 SLICES OF PARMA HAM, CUT INTO STRIPS 2 CM (¾ IN) WIDE

1 TEASPOON WALNUT OIL

½ TABLESPOON SNIPPED CHIVES

SALT AND FRESHLY GROUND BLACK PEPPER

FOR THE MUSTARD DRESSING:

1 TABLESPOON DIJON MUSTARD

1 TABLESPOON WHITE WINE VINEGAR

5 TABLESPOONS EXTRA VIRGIN OLIVE OIL

METHOD

If using the larger scallops, slice them horizontally into 2 discs. Leave queen scallops whole. Season with a little salt and pepper and set aside.

To make the croûtons, melt 25 g (1 oz) of the butter in a frying pan, add the cubes of bread and fry for a few minutes, turning them over as they brown. Lift out and drain on kitchen paper.

For the mustard dressing, whisk together the Dijon mustard and white wine vinegar, then gradually whisk in the olive oil and season with salt and pepper. Set aside.

Arrange the salad leaves on 4 warmed plates. Heat the frying pan until very hot and melt the remaining butter in it, then add the sliced scallops and fry for just 30 seconds on each side. Remove from the pan and tuck them in amongst the salad leaves. Add the strips of Parma ham and the croûtons to the pan and fry briskly over a high heat for just a few seconds to warm through. Sprinkle them over the salad. Now add the mustard dressing and walnut oil to the pan. Bring to the boil, stir in the chives and taste for seasoning. Drizzle over the salads and serve immediately.

sautéed scallops with caramelized chicory

The sweetness of scallops goes well with the slight bitterness of chicory, particularly when the chicory is lightly browned and slightly crisp around the edges.

SERVES 4

10 GOOD-SIZED PREPARED SCALLOPS (SEE P. 8)

6 SMALL HEADS OF CHICORY

100 G (4 OZ) UNSALTED BUTTER

120 ML (4 FL OZ) *FISH STOCK* (SEE P. 140) OR *CHICKEN STOCK* (SEE P. 140)

JUICE OF ½ LEMON

1 TEASPOON CHOPPED PARSLEY

SALT AND FRESHLY GROUND WHITE PEPPER

METHOD

Slice the scallops horizontally in half.

Remove the outer leaves of the chicory if they are damaged. Trim the base if it is brown but don't cut off too much or the leaves will detach themselves from the base. Cut them lengthways through the base into 3 thin slices.

Melt 25 g (1 oz) of the butter in a large frying pan. As soon as it starts to turn brown and smell slightly nutty, add the scallop slices and cook briefly for about 30 seconds on each side. Remove from the pan and keep warm.

Add a little more butter to the pan if necessary and fry a batch of chicory slices for about 1 minute on each side, until lightly browned. Transfer to another plate and keep warm while you cook the rest.

Add the stock and remaining butter to the pan, bring to the boil and boil until the sauce is thick enough to coat the back of a spoon. Add the lemon juice, season with a little salt and pepper and stir in the chopped parsley.

To serve, put the chicory on 4 warmed plates, top with the scallops and then spoon over the sauce.

basic recipes

kachumber salad

For 4 people, thinly slice 450 g (1 lb) of well-flavoured salad tomatoes. Cut 1 medium red onion into quarters lengthways and then thinly slice across. Layer in a shallow dish with 2 tablespoons of roughly chopped coriander, ¼ teaspoon of ground cumin, a good pinch of cayenne pepper, 1 tablespoon of white wine vinegar and ¼ teaspoon of salt. Serve straight away with any Indian-style dishes.

fish stock

MAKES 1.2 LITRES (2 PINTS)

1 KG (2¼ LB) FISH BONES SUCH AS LEMON
   SOLE, BRILL AND PLAICE

1 ONION, CHOPPED

1 BULB OF FENNEL, CHOPPED

100 G (4 OZ) CELERY, SLICED

100 G (4 OZ) CARROT, CHOPPED

25 G (1 OZ) BUTTON MUSHROOMS, SLICED

A SPRIG OF THYME

Put the fish bones and 2.25 litres (4 pints) of water into a large pan, bring just to the boil and simmer very gently for 20 minutes.

Strain through a muslin-lined sieve into a clean pan, add the vegetables and the thyme and bring back to the boil. Simmer for 35 minutes or until reduced to about 1.2 litres (2 pints).

Strain once more and use or store as required.

chicken stock

MAKES 1.7 LITRES (3 PINTS)

BONES FROM A 1.5 KG (3 LB) UNCOOKED
   CHICKEN OR 450 G (1 LB) CHICKEN WINGS

1 LARGE CARROT, CHOPPED

2 CELERY STICKS, SLICED

2 LEEKS, SLICED

2 BAY LEAVES

2 SPRIGS OF THYME

2.25 LITRES (4 PINTS) WATER

Put all the ingredients into a large pan and bring just to the boil, skimming off any scum from the surface as it appears. Leave to simmer very gently for 2 hours – it is important not to let it boil as this will force the fat from even the leanest chicken and make the stock cloudy.

Strain the stock through a muslin-lined sieve and use as required. If not using immediately, leave to cool, then chill and refrigerate or freeze for later use.

basic court bouillon

6 BAY LEAVES

1 TEASPOON BLACK PEPPERCORNS

1 CARROT, SLICED

1 SMALL ONION, SLICED

2 TABLESPOONS SALT

4 TABLESPOONS WHITE WINE VINEGAR

3.4 LITRES (6 PINTS) WATER

Put all the ingredients into a saucepan or fish kettle, bring to the boil and simmer for 20 minutes. You can set the court bouillon aside or chill at this stage until needed. Bring back to the boil before using.

court bouillon for poaching smoked fish

MAKES 900 ML (1½ PINTS)

300 ML (10 FL OZ) MILK

600 ML (1 PINT) WATER

1 MEDIUM ONION, THINLY SLICED

2 BAY LEAVES

6 PEPPERCORNS

½ LEMON, SLICED

Place all the ingredients in a pan and bring to the boil. Simmer for 10 minutes before using to poach the fish.

hollandaise sauce

SERVES 4

2 EGG YOLKS

225 G (8 OZ) *CLARIFIED BUTTER* (SEE P. 142),
   WARMED

JUICE OF ½ LEMON

A GOOD PINCH OF CAYENNE PEPPER

¾ TEASPOON SALT

Put the egg yolks and 2 tablespoons of water into a stainless-steel or glass bowl set over a pan of simmering water, making sure that the base of the bowl is not touching the water. Whisk until voluminous and creamy.

Remove the bowl from the pan and gradually whisk in the clarified butter until thick. Then whisk in the lemon juice, cayenne pepper and salt.

NOTE This sauce is best used as soon as it is made but will hold for up to 2 hours if kept covered in a warm place, such as over a pan of warm water.

quick hollandaise sauce

Using the same quantities as for hollandaise sauce, (see above) put the egg yolks, lemon juice and water into a liquidizer. Turn on the machine and then slowly pour in the warm butter through the lid. Season with cayenne pepper and salt.

mayonnaise

This recipe includes instructions for making mayonnaise in a liquidizer or food processor or by hand. It is lighter when made mechanically because the process uses a whole egg and is very quick. You can use either sunflower oil, olive oil or a mixture of the two if you prefer. It will keep in the fridge for up to 1 week.

MAKES 300 ML (10 FL OZ)

2 EGG YOLKS OR 1 EGG

2 TEASPOONS WHITE WINE VINEGAR

½ TEASPOON SALT

300 ML (10 FL OZ) SUNFLOWER OIL OR OLIVE OIL

TO MAKE THE MAYONNAISE BY HAND:
Make sure all the ingredients are at room temperature before you start. Put the egg yolks, vinegar and salt into a mixing bowl and then rest the bowl on a cloth to stop it slipping. Lightly whisk to break the yolks.

Using a wire whisk, beat the oil into the egg mixture a few drops at a time until you have incorporated it all. (Once you have added the same volume of oil as the original mixture of egg yolks and vinegar, you can add the oil a little more quickly.)

TO MAKE THE MAYONNAISE IN A MACHINE:
Put the whole egg, vinegar and salt into a liquidizer or food processor. Turn on the machine and slowly add the oil through the hole in the lid to make a thick emulsion.

marie rose sauce

Stir 5 tablespoons tomato ketchup, 4 tablespoons Greek-style natural yoghurt and some salt and freshly ground white pepper into 1 quantity *Mayonnaise* made with sunflower oil.

mustard mayonnaise

Make the mayonnaise in a liquidizer or food processor using a whole egg, 1 tablespoon white wine vinegar, 1 tablespoon English mustard, ¾ teaspoon salt, a little white pepper and sunflower oil.

aïoli

MAKES 175 ML (6 FL OZ)

4 GARLIC CLOVES, PEELED

½ TEASPOON SALT

1 MEDIUM EGG YOLK

2 TEASPOONS LEMON JUICE

175 ML (6 FL OZ) EXTRA VIRGIN OLIVE OIL

Put the garlic cloves on to a chopping board and crush them under the blade of a large knife. Sprinkle them with the salt and then work them with the knife blade into a smooth paste.

Scrape the garlic paste into a bowl and add the egg yolk and lemon juice. Using an electric hand mixer, whisk everything together and then very gradually whisk in the olive oil to make a thick mayonnaise-like mixture.

tartare sauce

½ QUANTITY MUSTARD MAYONNAISE (SEE ABOVE)

1 TEASPOON FINELY CHOPPED GREEN OLIVES

1 TEASPOON FINELY CHOPPED GHERKINS

1 TEASPOON FINELY CHOPPED CAPERS

2 TEASPOONS CHOPPED CHIVES

2 TEASPOONS CHOPPED PARSLEY

Mix together all the ingredients and serve.

goan masala paste

1 TEASPOON CUMIN SEEDS

1 TEASPOON CORIANDER SEEDS

1 TEASPOON BLACK PEPPERCORNS

½ TEASPOON FENNEL SEEDS

½ TEASPOON CLOVES

½ TEASPOON TURMERIC POWDER

50 G (2 OZ) MEDIUM-HOT RED DUTCH CHILLIES,
   ROUGHLY CHOPPED

½ TEASPOON SALT

3 GARLIC CLOVES, CHOPPED

1 TEASPOON LIGHT MUSCOVADO SUGAR

1½ TEASPOONS *TAMARIND WATER* (SEE RIGHT)

2.5 CM (1 IN) FRESH ROOT GINGER,
   ROUGHLY CHOPPED

1 TABLESPOON RED WINE VINEGAR

Grind the first 5 spices to a fine powder in a spice grinder. Put them into a food processor with the rest of the ingredients and blend to a smooth paste.

tapenade

MAKES 1 SMALL JAR

75 G (3 OZ) PITTED BLACK OLIVES, DRAINED
   AND RINSED

4 ANCHOVY FILLETS IN OLIVE OIL, DRAINED

25 G (1 OZ) CAPERS, WELL DRAINED AND RINSED

3 GARLIC CLOVES

85 ML (3 FL OZ) OLIVE OIL

FRESHLY GROUND BLACK PEPPER

Put the olives, anchovies, capers and garlic into a food processor and pulse 3 or 4 times. Then turn the processor on and add the oil in a thin steady stream through the lid.

Stir in black pepper to taste, spoon the mixture into a sterilized glass jar, seal and store in the fridge for up to 3 months. Use as required.

clarified butter

Place the butter in a small pan and leave it over a very low heat until it has melted. Then skim off any scum from the surface and pour off the clear (clarified) butter into a bowl, leaving behind the milky white solids that will have settled on the bottom of the pan.

tamarind water

Take a piece of tamarind pulp about the size of a tangerine and put it in a bowl with 150 ml (5 fl oz) of warm water. Work the paste into the water with your fingers until it has broken down and all the seeds have been released. Strain the slightly syrupy mixture through a fine sieve into another bowl and discard the fibrous material left in the sieve. The water is now ready to use and will store in the fridge for 24 hours.

shallot vinegar

85 ML (3 FL OZ) RED WINE

85 ML (3 FL OZ) RED WINE VINEGAR

1 SHALLOT, FINELY CHOPPED

Mix together all the ingredients.

index